THE AWFUL TRUTH ABOUT CAREERS IN REAL ESTATE

Copyright © 2017 George W. Mantor

All rights reserved. This book or any portion thereof may not be reproduced or used in any manner whatsoever without the express written permission of the publisher except for the use of brief quotations in a book review.

ISBN: 978-0-9989847-0-4

Front Cover Design by Jackie Miller: millerjackiej@gmail.com

Forward by Terri Murphy - terri@terrimurphy.com

Printed in the United States of America

THE AWFUL TRUTH ABOUT CAREERS IN REAL ESTATE
AND WHAT TO DO ABOUT IT

A GUIDE TO BUILDING A REWARDING REAL ESTATE BUSINESS

BY GEORGE W. MANTOR, THE REAL ESTATE PROFESSOR

CONTENTS

Foreword 1

Introduction 4
    Defining the Challenge 4
    The Pay is Terrible 5
    It is Harder Than It Looks 6
    View What You Do as Creating and Operating a Business 8
    A Word About People 12

Chapter 1: The Duties and Responsibilities of a
Real Estate Practitioner 14
    Functionary Duties 15
    Compliance Duties 15
    Fiduciary Duties 16
    Essential Competencies 17
    Five Key Attributes of Masters 19
        1. Commitment 19
        2. Perseverance 20
        3. Consistency 20
        4. Optimism 20
        5. Accountability 21
    Consumer Expectations 22
        Courtesy 22
        Thorough needs analysis 22
        Market analysis 23
        Strategy 23
        Advice and counsel 23
        Prior inspections 24
        Comparable market analysis (CMA) 24
        Mortgage review 25
        Title review 25
        Estimate of net proceeds 25
        Review escrow/closing instructions 25

Chapter 2: Ten Important Ideas 28
Build Value in Yourself 28
Create Your Perfect Customer 29
    Learn what to say 32
Identify and Develop Your Unique Skills and Talents....................... 32
Get a Marketable Listing in the Community That You Want to Dominate 33
Understand Where Opportunity Comes From................................. 35
Select the Right Community... 37
    Newer construction provides a great door opener for you 38
Exploit the Open House Opportunity 38
Guard Your Reputation 39
Achieve Your Full Potential Doing Things You Enjoy....................... 40
Technology and Social Media Will Not Save You 41
    Database (Community)...42
    Website...42

Chapter 3: The Ethical Business Model 43
The Activity – From Prospecting to Selecting...................................... 43
The Objective – From Lead Generation to Referral Creation 43
The Arena – From Geography to Community 44
The Role – From Salesperson to Trusted Advisor 46
The Relationship – From Functionary to Fiduciary 46
The Service – From Selling to Counseling... 47
The Pace – From Your Timetable to the Client's Timetable 47
The Process – From Promotion to Attraction...................................... 48
The Focus – From First-Time Buyers to First-Time Sellers 49
The Change – From External to Internal... 49
The Goal – From Making Money to Achieving Mastery...................... 50

Chapter 4: The Business Plan.. 52
Fifteen Simple Steps: What to Do, How to Do It, and Why................. 53
    1. Get a clear focus 54
    2. Evaluate the marketplace...55
    3. Analyze the competition..56
    4. Set realistic, specific and measurable goals, objectives, milestones and targets.. 57
    5. Define your market...58

  6. Develop your strategy 59
  7. Create your marketing plan 60
  8. Schedule the implementation of the plan 62
  9. Launch the plan 62
  10. Review, analyze, re-launch 62
  11. Differentiate 63
  12. Develop your brand 63
  13. Build a database 63
  14. Implement systems to ensure consistency 63
  15. Submit to coaching/consulting 63

Chapter 5: Selecting the Right Broker 65
 Identity 65
 What to Look For in a Brokerage 68
  1. Stability 68
  2. Reputation 68
  3. Training 68
  4. Location 69
  5. Experienced leadership 69
  6. Listings 69

Chapter 6: Effective Communication is Your Business 70
 The Importance of Clear Communication 70
 Factors Influencing Verbal Communication 72
 Factors Influencing Non-Verbal Communication 73
 Steps to Becoming a Great Communicator 74
 Recent Innovations in Technology and Unintended Consequences ... 76
  Why are you yelling at my voicemail? 76
  What if someone else is listening? 76
  Listen to the outgoing message to make sure you have the right person .76
  Precede and end every message by slowly stating your phone number ...77
  You've got mail 77
  Gr8 deal 4 u boi 77
  The blog cometh. Be afraid; be very afraid. 77
  Facebook follies 78
  Social networking has its place, but it also has its perils 78
  Celebs tweet a lot. Should you? 78

Chapter 7: The Principles of Negotiation 79
   Negotiation Skills 80

Chapter 8: Effectively Marketing Your Brand 83
   The Difference Between Sales and Marketing and Why it Matters 84
      Marketing and advertising are not synonymous 85
   Branding 86
      Defining the result 89
   First-Time Seller 89
   Identifying the Target Market 89
   Incorporating Your Uniqueness and Strengths Into the Brand 90
      Seize a niche 90
      Consider a slogo 90
      Avoid logo conflict 90
      Clever, not corny 91
      Junk is not marketing 91
   Consumer Education Imparts Real Value 91
   Presentations and Dialogues 92

Chapter 9: Building Listing Inventory 95
   Five Reasons Your Entire Focus Should be on Obtaining Listings 95
      Five marketable listings 96
      The importance of proper pricing 97
   The Critical Role of the CMA 97
      Factors to consider when selecting your community 99
   Three Things You Can Control 100
      Focus on listings 100
      Say the phrase that pays 100
      Gear all marketing to the pursuit of listing referrals 101
   Setting and Preparing for the Appointment 101
      Setting the perfect price 102
      Organize the presentation 102
   It's Showtime! 104

Chapter 10: An Open House With a Purpose 108
   Select the Right Community 108
   Select the Right Home 109
   Ensure Success 110

Sign Psychology 111
At the Open House 112
    Guest book 112
    Display 112
    Food 113
    Loan officer 113
    Handout 113

Chapter 11: Serving Real Estate Buyers 114
The Initial Consultation 115
Ask Questions, Shut Up, and Listen 115
Prequalification 119
Show New Homes First 121
The Story of Discovery Hills 122
Showings 123
Photo Album 124
Toolkit 125
Setting the Order 125
Writing the Offer 126
    Where? 126
Getting to the Bottom Line 127
Presenting the Offer 128

Chapter 12: Predictable Obstacles to Closing and How to Avoid Them 130
Dealing With Uncertainty 131
Elements of an Initial Consultation 132
    Needs analysis 132
    The bigger picture 132
    Demographics 133
    Local market conditions 134
    Paperwork review 134
    Closing process step-by-step 134
    Milestones 135
    Communication 135

Chapter 13: Distressed Property, Short Sales, Foreclosures, and REOs 136
Title Problems, MERS, and Void Assignments 138

Short Sales 139
Real Estate Owned (REOs) 140
Foreclosures 140
    Foreclosure process 141
    Stopping the foreclosure sale 143
    After the foreclosure 143

Chapter 14: Stress and Your Health 145
Repeat Positive Affirmations 149
Eat Healthy 150
Keep Moving 153
Make a List of Everything You Enjoy Doing 155

Chapter 15: What to Wear 157
Basic Wardrobe for Men 159

Chapter 16: Money, Money, Money 160
The Modern Global Monetary Farce 163
    Money is debt 163
    You have no money in the bank 164
    There is no money 164
    Banks create virtual money when someone borrows it 165
Fiat Currency 167
Fractional Reserve Banking 168
    Every dollar borrowed is worth $10 to the bank 168
    The Federal Reserve 168
    Shadow banking 170
Massive Mortgaged-Backed Securities Fraud 172
    Mortgages designed by risk experts to increase defaults to record levels 173
Understanding the Economy 174
Virtual Money 178
The Abolishment of Cash 179

Chapter 17: Each and Every Day, Better in Every Way 182
Never Look Back and Wonder What Might Have Been 184
If You Do Something Often Enough, You Will Get Good at It 191
Keeping the Faith 197

Chapter 18: The Possibilities are Endless 199

Reinvention is the Spice of Life 200
    "Annyeong-haseyo?" 201
Mercury Rising: A Case Study in Market Analysis 201
    Defining the challenges 202
    Learning the hard way 203
Nothing is Perfect 205
Project Analysis 207
    Strengths 208
    Changing Functions Drive Changing Form 213
Strategy 217
    Advertising 217
    Signage 217
    Flex walls 218
    Reaching out to the brokers and agents 218
    Seller financing 218
    "Plan B" the builder's "spec lock" 219
    Bulk sale 220

Conclusion 222
Appendix A 231
Appendix B 232
Appendix C 233
Appendix D 245
About the Author 253

FOREWORD
by Terri Murphy

Did you happen to notice that everyone appears different? Different from you, your values, your perceptions, your preferences, your culture, your style... yup... everyone is different.

One of the most magnificent elements of life in the physical is that when we celebrate these differences and revel in the fresh or different perspectives from another's experiences, we arrive at a new level of introspection and ultimately a high level of collaboration. Seeing the world through the eyes and experiences of another is a goldmine if you know how and why to seek it out.

When it comes to any entrepreneurial endeavor, being unique is not only required, it is paramount to branding, positioning, messaging, and delivery of our product or services. What makes us "different from" is the special sauce — the incredibly unique gift we bring to the universe we live in. These differences are gifts from our creator to sustain us, to guide us, and to bring meaning to our lives as well as propel us in our endeavors.

As a long time real estate practitioner and author of several books on real estate, I was intrigued by the title, "The Awful Truth About Careers in Real Estate," by 40-year-old real estate veteran, George W. Mantor.

As a coach with a "make lemonade from lemons attitude," the title of his book made me pause. His book presents an alternative paradigm to what he might call the "Glengarry Glen Ross" model of lead generation, selling, and closing that has been common throughout the real estate industry for decades.

Instead, George advocates focusing exclusively on listing, and in particular, following a system to create a 100 percent referral business; an almost identical parallel in strategy for how I listed and sold close to 100 properties a year for most of my career.

He points to the high failure rate of new practitioners as a symptom of a business model that hasn't kept up with the pace of change in other areas of our lives. Backed by research, George points out that the typical length of a consumer buying or selling experience exceeds four years, or about twice as long as a new agent's career.

The largest consumer segment of property purchases is found in the GenX/Y/Millennial quadrant. This group doesn't value experience as much as they demand a "good real estate experience" during the process. A standard approach to buying and selling won't get the referrals needed to build a community of raving fans, so George set out to show practitioners exactly how to do it.

In his book, George emphasizes viewing real estate as the business it is and not simply a "sales job."

We know from our experience in our company that a professional is incapable of working beyond their skill set, so the key to growth is a relentless commitment to learning and self-improvement.

His fresh view urges real estate agents to build their business in the pursuit of activities they actually enjoy, thereby allowing them to effortlessly incorporate their uniqueness into their business. This assures a community of likeminded people who would naturally want to help you. As he points out, you cannot achieve your full potential doing things you do not enjoy.

This approach demands a focus on a high degree of ethics since the only person you really compete with is yourself. A great reputation as a person who happens to be a professional, supported by a community of raving fans, is the lifeblood of a referral business.

FOREWORD

George provides an easy to follow plan that assures that you will be doing the most important activities at all times. Do them regularly and results will follow.

And like only George can do, he peppers the content with interesting real world stories and great tips that are perfect for the plugged in generation.

The book contains an entire chapter on open houses. I know, as does George, that most agents waste their time and energy producing a standard event when in fact, the opportunity for branding and connection can be off the charts when an open house is executed with a premium marketing plan to produce stellar outcomes.

George's sense of humor is fun, funny, and inspiring. His gift to the reader is his immense passion for the business, the curiosity to ask "what if," and the sharing of his wisdom and expertise with those that are willing to look at the industry from a new perspective.
-Terri Murphy

Terri Murphy is the CIO of U.S. Learning, LLC, located in Memphis helping corporations, associations, and entrepreneurs improve their bottom line through one-on-one consulting strategies. As a top producing sales agent in the Chicago area for over 24 years, Terri Murphy listed and sold over 100 homes a year without a team and when interest rates soared to double digits.

She is a best-selling author of five books on real estate sales success and leadership, as well as a columnist, online television producer, and business e-communication consultant. Most recently, she was a contributing author to "Trump: The Best Real Estate Advice I Ever Received."

INTRODUCTION

"Things are not always what they seem; the first appearance deceives many; the intelligence of a few perceives what has been carefully hidden." —PHAEDRUS

DEFINING THE CHALLENGE

Are you considering a career in real estate? It seems almost everyone wonders at some point if they should "get into real estate."

Be your own boss, set your own hours, drive a fancy car, and earn what you are really worth. Good jobs are hard to find. Most new jobs are low wage and part time. Many talented people have been forced to consider other ways of getting by, and it seems almost everyone mulls over a real estate career at one time or another. How about you?

Do you have what it takes to earn a living in a highly competitive and legally constrained arena like real estate? Probably not. The deck is definitely stacked against you, and only a small percentage of new licensees ever bother to renew their licenses when they expire.

The problem is not the economy as much as it is an excess of practitioners well beyond what the number of transactions can support. Imagine the result of opening the same sandwich shop on every corner. The company would sell a lot of sandwiches, but the individual owners would all go broke. That is the business model for real estate; address the high failure rate by bringing ever more people into the business.

INTRODUCTION

THE PAY IS TERRIBLE

The real estate business can hardly be thought of as a lucrative endeavor, and the chances of any real success are limited by the excess of practitioners all competing for business they will not be receiving. If you do what they do, you will get the results they are getting.

Are you sitting down? According to the "2017 National Association of Realtors® Member Profile," members in the business two years or less had a median gross income of $8,930 in 2016. That's the median, meaning that half of them earned less. Expenses were $6,000. A paper route would be more profitable.

Why is the pay so bad, you may wonder? The answer is the business version of the natural selection process; sadly, inexperienced real estate agents are earning exactly what they are worth — next to nothing.

If you can survive the first two years, it gets better, but not much, the median income for licensed salespersons was $31,670. Subtract their business expenses and their pretax profit is just above the poverty line for a family of four.

The median for all NAR members including brokers was $69,640.

However, those in business for more than 16 years earned $78,850 and had 15 transactions as opposed to the typical agent who had 12. Not only does their volume increase, but they earn more than twice as much per closing than less experienced members.

But, before you jump to the conclusion that longevity is the secret rather than value, brokers typically earn about twice that of an experienced salesperson. Those members willing to invest time and money to advance in their profession by obtaining a broker's license are likely to further expand their knowledge through other avenues.

It is apparent that the combination of experience derived from tenure and knowledge attained through self-improvement lead to more and better business.

Now you know the truth. The million-dollar real estate agent is a myth. But, it perpetuates an unending supply of wanna-be-wealthy new licensees, 95 percent of whom are doomed to failure because there is not enough business to support them, and more seasoned agents are already burrowed deep into the minds of many potential clients.

Do not be tempted to think that your experience will be any different. It is not you. Failing to gain a foothold in the real estate business is not the result of laziness or stupidity. Many ambitious, highly intelligent people wash out of real estate. Residential real estate is not difficult, but neither is it what it appears to be. It is not a job of selling; it is about asking well-thought-out questions and listening carefully to the answers.

IT IS HARDER THAN IT LOOKS

I started out in the real estate business back in 1978; we were just referred to as "warm bodies," or my personal favorite, "fodder for the machine." We were new *recruits*, in every sense of the word. We were conscripted into the cause to fill the ranks of those who had fallen before us.

It would now be up to us to march forth into their abandoned "farms" and distribute material with the broker's name and phone number on it. We were cheaper than postage.

The criterion, as I would come to learn, is that we could make

INTRODUCTION

steam on a mirror. So, before you fall in love with all of those brokers courting you, that is what they do. Their business model is actually based on recruiting rather than retention, failure rather than success, quantity not quality. It acknowledges almost total failure of new licensees and responds by recruiting more.

The small number of agents who succeed get much higher commission splits and are often unprofitable for the broker. Fortunately for the broker, when it comes to real estate, failure is far more common than success. The vast majority of new licensees leave the business without ever closing a single transaction.

I know, nobody ever told you. Me neither. Not one word was ever said to me about the almost certain likelihood that I would fail out of the business within a year. No one told me that there were five times as many practitioners as the pace of closings can support.

What I remember was attending a career night in the fall of 1978 and an agent by the name of Judy Jackson leaping up from her desk proclaiming, "I made $9,000 last month." Making $108,000 per year in 1978 was living large. What I did not know was that Judy was an exceptional person and a wonderful lady who was well suited to the business.

Many people discover that they just do not like the many facets of the occupation. Some become embittered but stay in the business anyway if they can eke out a living. They can be very difficult to work with during the closing period. "Well that's your job," is a frequent response when trying to complete the numerous tasks in a timely fashion.

This line of work can be contentious and unpleasant, and it is necessary, occasionally, to politely assert oneself while keeping emotions and personal feelings in check. This is not easy for everyone. Attitude and focus are critical. For us to get paid, a closing must occur, and that is what we are engaged to achieve. Who does what and personal feeling are irrelevant.

If you are a new licensee or considering a career in real estate, you are probably haunted by one nagging question, "How do I make money?"

You don't! But, you can make friends, and if you make enough friends, opportunities will flow to you. If you are well prepared, those opportunities will lead to money and satisfaction.

Rather than spend months preparing for something that does not exist, why not first analyze the reality of the arena. Then with an understanding of the true impediments to success, plan a course to militate against them.

VIEW WHAT YOU DO AS CREATING AND OPERATING A BUSINESS

Whether you are a single agent, a team, or a mega corporation, you are in business where business principles apply. The language of business is numbers, and if you know your numbers, you can influence the direction of your business.

The numbers that matter most to you are the size of your personal sphere of influence (or community), the number of referral sources, the dollar value of your current inventory and the dollar value of your pipeline.

When we used to think of communities, we thought of geographic areas like towns or neighborhoods. While those are part of your sphere of influence, your community extends to everyone you know considering anyone, anywhere, at any time of day could send you a referral.

INTRODUCTION

In addition to the size of your community, an important number to track is the number of people who have promised to send you referrals. For anyone to be counted in this group, you must have had a sit-down, face-to-face meeting for the specific purpose of them committing to send you referrals.

Everyone who has expressed an interest in buying or selling real estate comprises your inventory. This predicts your future income and serves as a reminder of where to spend your valuable time moving them to your pipeline.

The fourth important number is the value of your pipeline. These are pending transactions.

Faithfully tracking those four numbers is critical in your success because they drive your daily activities. No matter how hard you work, if you are doing the wrong things for the wrong reasons, you are doomed. If you are not meeting new people regularly, having referral source meetings daily, moving your inventory or managing your pipeline, you are not running your business properly.

The primary reasons for failure are lack of focus on the things that matter and an inability to inspire confidence. Looking for easy deals is not being focused, it is fishing. You are not trying to talk anyone into anything — you are fostering a relationship. That may or may not lead to business, but it sure can't hurt.

Improve your odds by planning, organizing, directing, and controlling your business using the same methods and philosophies driving today's most successful businesses. I have been in real estate management or brokerage ownership of one form or another since 1980, and my entire focus has been helping others achieve their goals by enhancing their natural talents and abilities. I created the <u>Personal Best System</u> to guide business owners on the journey to maximizing their unique talents and abilities.

THE AWFUL TRUTH ABOUT CAREERS IN REAL ESTATE AND WHAT TO DO ABOUT IT

The obstacle to building a real estate business is that most agents are simply replicating what they see others doing. Most of the training being done by real estate companies is insufficient and misdirected. They spend a fortune, and most will tell you privately that it does not appear to improve performance. They are simply being trained to do the wrong things.

See it as a business, not a sales job. Almost anyone of average intelligence can succeed if they approach it as creating and operating a business — a personal services business.

It is only a matter of creating a <u>simple</u> business plan and implementing it.

The purpose of this book is to provide a step-by-step guide to simple and effective methods for vastly improving your odds of building a business that is economically sufficient to meet your needs and wants, and is also personally satisfying because you know you are doing the right things in the right way.

There are a lot of real estate books out there, but most appear to be written by people who have not really been in the field. Hopefully, some of the stories I tell from my own experience will help you see the bigger picture.

I have incorporated that experience into the dozens of articles I have written for real estate publications. I created the "Real Estate Professor" to advance consumer and practitioner knowledge, host a radio program, and conduct community workshops.

My experience is in California, and there are customs and economic circumstances in other areas that may not be reflective of California. But wherever you are, the underlying principles still apply.

You will note that I will revisit some of those essential themes throughout the book because many of them are counter to

INTRODUCTION

what you will observe within the industry. They may seem counterintuitive, but that is simply because real estate, consumer's expectations and methods of communication have changed dramatically while the industry still plods along in the 50s with sales contests and lead generation programs.

I know most real estate practitioners will not read this book, which is to your advantage. Many brokers, owners and managers will reject this approach because they are unprepared to support it. They still believe that it is a selling occupation, and yet the consumer has clearly indicated that they prefer a consultative relationship where information, trust, confidence, and ability are at the center, rather than a commission check.

Can you be one of the few who actually creates a rewarding business or will you spend your time prospecting for leads to sell and close?

If you follow the methods revealed in this book, you will eliminate virtually any competition because you will have created a unique community of 20,000 people from which business flows to you.

If you commit to becoming a master of the essential competencies of real estate services, potential clients will be comparing you favorably to other practitioners they may know, and they will be referring you to their community.

If you want to build a business that is fun and profitable, then strive to achieve your personal best and track the numbers that matter. If you do that, the army of know-nothing salespeople will be an asset, not a liability.

I have never worried about losing a potential client; in fact, I often cannot get rid of them.

A WORD ABOUT PEOPLE

People, not real estate, are your business. You can use this business model to build any personal services business. If you do not have compassion and empathy for others, you cannot fake it. Buying or selling real estate is simply the response to a major event taking place in a person's life; it is not an isolated event.

Always be cordial. I grew up on the Mesabi Iron Range near Bovey, Minnesota, and we did not see many people. Everyone was interesting. Going into Grand Rapids for provisions was a social event. In cities today, people are throw-aways; I notice that when I go out most people try to ignore everyone they encounter, whereas I see opportunities to connect, even if for only a moment.

If you do not really like people, you should consider other career options.

Real estate can be an extremely rewarding and personally fulfilling way to spend your life, or it could be the worst experience you will ever have, depending on how you go about it.

If you want to build a business around the things you enjoy with friends you make, this book is essential to your success. This is your indispensable guide, your workbook, and the chapters will explain step-by-step what you need to succeed.

The following is sometimes attributed to Mother Teresa but the author is Kent M. Keith:

INTRODUCTION

People are illogical, unreasonable, and self-centered.
Love them anyway.

If you do good, people will accuse you of selfish ulterior motives.
Do good anyway.

If you are successful, you will win false friends and true enemies.
Succeed anyway.

The good you do today will be forgotten tomorrow.
Do good anyway.

Honesty and frankness make you vulnerable.
Be honest and frank anyway.

The biggest men and women with the biggest ideas can be shot down by the smallest men and women with the smallest minds.
Think big anyway.

People favor underdogs but follow only top dogs.
Fight for a few underdogs anyway.

What you spend years building may be destroyed overnight.
Build anyway.

People really need help but may attack you if you do help them.
Help people anyway.

Give the world the best you have and you'll get kicked in the teeth.
Give the world the best you have anyway.

CHAPTER 1

THE DUTIES AND RESPONSIBILITIES OF A REAL ESTATE PRACTITIONER

"No one can achieve their full potential doing things they don't enjoy."
—G.W. MANTOR

The majority of people who enter the real estate business have only a vague idea of what they will actually be doing day to day. Once they come to learn the reality of the business, they are often disillusioned because they do not really have the temperament needed to enjoy the work.

A competent, knowledgeable real estate practitioner gets paid for their time and their knowledge. If they have little knowledge, their time is not very valuable.

Everyone's time is limited. At some point, in the development of a personal service business, practitioners can work no more hours. And, as they build their business, enhance their skills and improve their knowledge, they can only increase their compensation by increasing their fees or adding additional revenue streams. Remember, the very best in every profession are almost always the best compensated.

Given the flood of inexperienced recruits who enter the field each year, a strong argument can be made that they should be paid what they are worth, and as noted in the introduction, according to the "2017 National Association of Realtors® Member Profile," members in the business two years or less had a median gross income of $8,930.

THE DUTIES AND RESPONSIBILITIES OF A REAL ESTATE PRACTITIONER

Understanding the value of a real estate practitioner is made more difficult by what the consumer sees and does not see.

From what I gather, a common perception of a real estate practitioner is someone who drives around in an expensive car, holds open houses, has a list of "for sale" properties and a special key, puts up "Sold" signs, talks incessantly, demonstrates few social graces, scans the room over your shoulder looking for someone better to go get pushy with, and gets paid millions for doing the above.

And, to all of this, we add fuel by pretending to make more money than we actually do by boasting about our "million-dollar producers" as though earning $15,000 a year were an unusual achievement.

The work of a real estate practitioner can be broken down into three main categories: functionary duties, compliance duties and fiduciary duties.

FUNCTIONARY DUTIES

Most of what the public sees the practitioner doing could be described as functionary activities. Measuring a house, hanging a lock box, canvassing a neighborhood, and designing flyers are examples of things that could be done by a trained chimpanzee and, arguably, do not rise to the value of several thousand dollars.

COMPLIANCE DUTIES

Behind the scenes, the trend toward consumerism and subsequent government regulation have placed burdensome responsibilities on sellers of real property to such an extent that most sellers have no idea what disclosures are required of them or what the consequences are for failing to provide them.

Many sellers incorrectly believe that their agent is responsible for providing these disclosures, but the legal onus is upon the seller. Among the practitioner's compliance duties is a risk reduction strategy that directs the seller to be in compliance with all legally mandated requirements.

Over the course of my 39 years in real estate, I have watched a standard real estate contract swell from a couple of pages to a 3-pound bundle of disclosures, addenda, inspections, affidavits, disclaimers, waivers, reports, indemnifications, acknowledgements, and amendments. These are all woven together in a labyrinth of time frames, receipts, authorizations and approvals, all with their unique ramifications and consequences for buyers and sellers of real estate.

The fact that consumers do not see all this does not make it any less binding upon them.

For a real estate broker, these increasing compliance issues impact the cost of training, processing, filing, paper, toner, equipment, and long-term storage. It either gets paid for by the consumer or it does not get done. The consumer not in compliance is the one at risk, not the agent who cuts corners.

FIDUCIARY DUTIES

This brings us to what the public often does not see; the top professionals in any field exhibit qualities that come at a price. Often, they are very selective regarding the clients they accept. Experience and longevity create an existing clientele.

The fiduciary relationship is based on trust. There is an absolute duty of fairness and honesty. And, in my view, there is a duty of competence as well. That means education, training and a commitment to mastering all of the technical and legal nuances of the business.

THE DUTIES AND RESPONSIBILITIES OF A REAL ESTATE PRACTITIONER

Mastery. What does it mean? Is it a journey, or a destination? Is it mechanics or mindset? Does it even matter in the dog-eat-dog arena of real estate sales? In fact, from what I have observed, the pursuit of mastery is the only certain path to a rewarding career in any personal service business.

The better you do the things you do, the more people will talk about you. The more they talk about you, the more referrals you will get. The ultimate goal is a steady stream of listing referrals already predisposed to have you list their home.

And, so we ask ... mastery of what?

ESSENTIAL COMPETENCIES

Former chief economist of the National Association of Realtors, John Tucillo, identified what he believed to be the seven essential competencies of a real estate practitioner.

1. Counseling the consumer
2. Negotiating the contract
3. Managing the transaction
4. Marketing
5. Building and maintaining a brand
6. Acquiring, managing, and using information
7. Thinking strategically

There are three roads to choose from in real estate:

- You can choose to become a _master of the competencies_ and have your value speak for itself.
- You can take the road of prospecting, lead generating, and selling and closing, which requires you to become a _master of persuasion_. Or....
- Concede your lack of value, become _master of nothing_ and make working for less your value proposition.

THE AWFUL TRUTH ABOUT CAREERS IN REAL ESTATE AND WHAT TO DO ABOUT IT

The desire to become a *master of the competencies* can spring from considering the alternatives. I strongly recommend that you see the movie adaptation of David Mamet's Broadway play about real estate sales, *Glengarry Glen Ross*.

The characters' essential truth and yours are one in the same. Like Godot, the "good leads" are not coming… ever. No matter how many pages of full-color advertising your broker runs, the good leads just are not coming.

The road to mastery requires that you create your own customers and not have the building of your business be dependent on the number and quality of someone else's leads. If the leads are so good, how did they trickle down to you? Wake up! You must create your own customers. The methods you use to create your customers will determine your success and satisfaction owning a real estate business.

The road to mastery leaves nothing in doubt. You will do whatever it takes to ensure your success and nothing will stop you. Remember, in the pursuit of mastery, the destination and the journey are one in the same.

Think of someone you associate with the title "Master." See the certainty and practiced ease with which they approach their craft. Words like dexterity, grace, rhythm, and efficiency describe their movements.

With the proper attitude, you can become a *master of the real estate competencies* and build a satisfying and rewarding long-term, predictable business. But, it won't happen without a plan, knowledge, experience, and proper coaching.

Many extremely ambitious people fail in real estate. Hard work is not the answer. You cannot prospect harder. You cannot hold an open house harder. The key is to make it easier, not harder.

THE DUTIES AND RESPONSIBILITIES OF A REAL ESTATE PRACTITIONER

To make it effortless, it has to be fun. If real estate does not provide you with satisfaction, you cannot succeed. Note that professional athletes and performers are among the best-compensated people in our society and they are doing what they love to do. The love of an activity and a high level of proficiency go hand in hand. How can anyone achieve their full potential doing things they do not enjoy?

In the words of author James A. Michener:

"The master in the art of living makes little distinction between his work and his play, his love and his religion. He hardly knows which is which. He simply pursues his vision of excellence at whatever he does, leaving others to decide whether he is working or playing. To him, he's always doing both."

And, that is what is truly remarkable about the real estate business. If you approach it as a business, rather than a sales job, you can do what you most enjoy doing as a way to build a long-term cash flow.

FIVE KEY ATTRIBUTES OF MASTERS

Do you possess or can you develop the attributes of a master?

1. Commitment

Woody Allen once remarked that 80 percent of success was showing up. Showing up on time, every time demonstrates the commitment necessary to achieve mastery. A commitment is a promise that cannot be broken under any circumstances. It is either iron-clad or it is no commitment at all. If you say you will be there, you must be there. That means for clients, meetings, and training. When in doubt, always do what you have scheduled.

2. Perseverance

Nothing of value comes easily or quickly. The road to mastery is not free of obstacles; it is positively littered with them. It is the overcoming of those obstacles that galvanizes the will of the master to overcome even greater challenges and to push on after others have surrendered to exhaustion and despair. Most people give up before they are truly defeated. Nearly all limitations are ultimately self-imposed.

3. Consistency

Weight trainers say, "If you do the reps, you'll get the results."

Muscle is built one repetition at a time over a period of weeks. A 100 percent referral business is built one person at a time over a period of years. It is the day in and day out adherence to the activities in the plan that ultimately determines the growth and profitability of your business.

Every day should allow for some time specifically devoted to doing the "reps."

4. Optimism

Most people are negative by nature. As a business owner, you cannot afford negative thoughts. Maintain a focus on that over which you have influence — yourself. What are the messages you are sending yourself?

Everywhere I go I ask people how they are. I get a lot of "OK" and "Pretty good I guess" or even less enthusiastic responses. They feel obligated to ask me, and I shoot right back with a cheery "Never better!" The responses I get generally fall into one of three categories: Disbelief, denial or curiosity. It is a great conversation starter that often leads to the question, "What do you do?"

Self-development, training, and coaching will help you maintain your optimism. The right attitude is essential as you go through the normal and predictable struggles and disappointments associated with building a business in a highly competitive arena.

Pay attention to what you think and say. Pay attention to what you put into your body and how you treat it. It is difficult to be optimistic if you do not feel well. Move. Get out of that chair, get off of that couch, and get going. Your business needs someone who is strong, vibrant, energetic, and upbeat.

5. *Accountability*

Masters want and accept responsibility for their actions and their results. Because it is your business, it will be up to you to hold <u>you</u> accountable. At the first inkling that something is not working, do what a good businessperson would do and build in levels of accountability. Find someone to hold you accountable. Whether you call them a coach, broker, mentor, fellow professional, partner, or even a friend, their job is to hold the mirror.

Often when people do not like what they see, they fire the mirror holder. The master is open to all information without judgment and understands that much valuable wisdom can be passed along by those who have gone before them. A master honors the holder of the mirror. And, buys him a delicious lunch … in which case I am available for mirror holding.

A master always seeks to learn more, to grow more, to give more, and to have greater value in service to others. What sounds more exhilarating, becoming a master of the competencies, a master of persuasion, or a master of nothing at all?

CONSUMER EXPECTATIONS

In addition to the five key attributes, consumers should be able to expect the following from a top professional:

Courtesy

With privileged athletes and rock stars as our role models, boorish behavior has become mainstream. I am old school. I still believe in something called "professional conduct." I do not need a code of ethics or Dr. Phil to tell me how to conduct myself in my myriad of daily encounters with people.

A consumer of any product or service should expect, at minimum, that a true professional will always be well-mannered, polite, relaxed, patient, and empathetic. These are more than niceties; they are valuable assets that benefit the client. These attributes foster effective communication, which is the heart of better negotiation.

"Don't think twice, just be nice." Years ago, I heard a very popular real estate sales trainer say that the worst thing that people could think of you was that you were nice. I do not agree, but then again I am a country boy, and I was reared to be polite and considerate. Beyond that, being nice is just good business and is far more likely to positively contribute to a referral-only business. If people do not like you, they won't refer to you, and they won't call you in a crisis.

Courtesy extends to being on time, returning phone calls promptly, and fulfilling commitments.

Thorough needs analysis

Any professional will want to meet their client in their offices for the purpose of an initial consultation. The reasons for the meeting include determining if their situation fits your expertise, to

THE DUTIES AND RESPONSIBILITIES OF A REAL ESTATE PRACTITIONER

conduct a thorough analysis of their circumstances and options, and to make sure they fully understand the process.

I know very well that many real estate trainers suggest meeting the client in their home, but I have had better success bringing the client into a professional office where I have all of my tools and he or she can see that I am legitimate and credible.

This meeting should not only focus entirely on them, but also allow you an opportunity to break down all that will happen, where information comes from, and what it means to them.

This is a pre-listing meeting. If the meeting is executed as planned, the listing appointment can then focus entirely on pricing and marketing related to the property.

Market analysis

Only a well-informed buyer or seller can make the best decisions. They need to be fully aware of current market dynamics that could ultimately impact their choices. Knowing and presenting this information will be vital to your success.

Strategy

Once the consumer understands their options, the consumer and the professional can begin to form a plan for achieving the one best option for the consumer and their circumstances. Their best option could be doing something entirely different than their original plan, or even nothing at all. The strategy is the step-by-step process of achieving their best option.

Advice and counsel

It can be hard to appreciate the value here but, in my view, advice and counsel are probably of greatest value to the client. I once asked the agent representing the buyer of my listing, "What did you advise your client to do?"

His response was, "I don't give my clients advice."

Frankly, I was stunned. I have long found that one of the most valuable roles I played was to tell the client what my knowledge and experience suggest we do under the circumstances. In my view, a consumer who is not receiving informed advice should expect a discount.

Prior inspections

Most real estate professionals hate surprises. They understand that it is far better for the seller if all property defects are determined prior to bringing the property to market. Those defects will be discovered by the buyer's inspection, which is likely to trigger protracted and needlessly acrimonious renegotiation and often cancellation.

Comparable market analysis (CMA)

The key to selling quickly for the highest possible price is to place the property in the marketplace at exactly the right price. If the price is too high, the best qualified buyers will not get to see the property because they will be looking at homes priced in their spending range. A consumer should expect that their home will be priced properly so that legitimate buyers are not precluded from seeing it.

A consumer should expect to receive two sets of data to help determine current market value; this should include data on what buyers have recently paid for nearby properties that possess similar attributes, such as square footage and amenities, and data on what other options are available nearby.

It is critical that sellers fully understand the importance of proper pricing and what underlies that determination. The home is sold when it is priced properly to begin with. Buyers have the same data and will not buy an overpriced house.

THE DUTIES AND RESPONSIBILITIES OF A REAL ESTATE PRACTITIONER

Mortgage review

A seller should expect that a listing agent will conduct a mortgage review to determine if there is a prepayment penalty, balloon payment or other fees associated with paying off the mortgage. Sellers have been blindsided by these costs at closing.

Title review

There could be a lien on the property the seller does not know about until they attempt to sell. Considering that even one mistake will take time to unravel, this should be determined early on in the listing period.

Estimate of net proceeds

When a seller lists a home for sale, the only thing that matters to them is their net proceeds, not the selling price or the agent's commission. A seller should expect that any professional real estate practitioner would provide them with a breakdown of all the known and anticipated costs associated with selling real estate.

Review escrow/closing instructions

Once an offer has been accepted, the seller should expect that their escrow instructions have been fully reviewed prior to presentation for signature. The true professional wants to be certain that there are no surprises and that the instructions to the escrow company reflect the meeting of the minds of the parties. Usually, more than one party is contributing information to escrow, and they do not always get it right.

In many states, attorneys are involved in the closing process and may be presumed to have reviewed the closing documents as well as other documents associated with the transaction. In a perfect world, perhaps, but the true professional leaves nothing to chance.

THE AWFUL TRUTH ABOUT CAREERS IN REAL ESTATE AND WHAT TO DO ABOUT IT

The seller may never have spoken to the attorney leading up to and during the course of the transaction, and then there are the contributions of anywhere between 20 to 30 other participants, whose work product and generally payment are all coordinated in the closing documents.

If those 10 elements are missing, then (in my view) the consumer did not get full value from his agent. On the other hand, if the real estate professional was upbeat, on the ball, honest, caring and efficient, in my judgment, the seller received high quality, professional service and got his money's worth.

I have never advocated against those business models whose value proposition is discounted fees. Discounting brokers are hardly new to the marketplace, as much as they would like you to believe otherwise. They come and go as the market changes. They often serve as valuable training grounds for new licensees who are willing to work for less to offset their inexperience. In a few years, if properly tutored, these agents will have built enough value in themselves to justify top tier compensation. My bet is that they will not continue discounting once they have achieved mastery.

The real estate business has become so complex and legal that a meaningful apprenticeship ought to be required. However, the failure rate is so high and the turnover so rapid that it can be difficult to build much of a foundation of knowledge of real estate fundamentals while driving the salesperson to be a good closer. At least with discounting brokers the argument can be made that, "I don't know much about real estate, but I can save you thousands in fees."

I know it can sound trite to say "You get what you pay for," and, we all know from our own firsthand experiences with all manner of things, including real estate professionals, it is not always true. But, one thing is obvious — the best and the brightest will go where they are rewarded commensurate with their talent.

THE DUTIES AND RESPONSIBILITIES OF A REAL ESTATE PRACTITIONER

The consumer may save money, but the service level will fall as well. And, a handful of the very best will increase their fees in recognition of their higher level of service. Brokerage fees are negotiable and they should be. At the same time, the best should earn the most. Go the extra mile, charge a premium for service, and know that some people want the top-of-the-line no matter the cost.

The skills required to master the real estate profession are easily transferable to other arenas. If the dumb-down factor becomes so great that masters cannot earn a living in real estate, they will just switch to another business.

In the words of Oscar Wilde, *"I have the simplest tastes. I am always satisfied with the best."*

Your duty and your responsibility are to become the best — the very best that you can be.

CHAPTER 2

TEN IMPORTANT IDEAS

"Take up one idea. Make that one idea your life. Think of it, dream of it, live on that idea. Let the brain, muscles, nerves, every part of your body, be full of that idea, and just leave every other idea alone. This is the way to success. That is way great spiritual giants are produced."
—SWAMI VIVEKANANDA

Everything begins with an idea; a moment perhaps when we either see something entirely new or see something in a new way. A business thrives on ideas and 10 is nowhere near too many. The journey is lifelong and there is no destination, just new ideas.

BUILD VALUE IN YOURSELF

He who grows fastest wins. What value do you have if you are brand new to the business? License preparation has nothing to do with succeeding in business nor does it warrant the same compensation as seasoned veterans who are highly knowledgeable and well-skilled. Outsiders underestimate the learning curve of what is a highly complex legal, financial, emotional, and astonishingly competitive business.

Your radiant smile, your essential goodness as a human being, and your "love of houses," will be of little help without a deep and abiding commitment to continual self-improvement. You will only get referrals if people have confidence in you.

You must demonstrate your value. With so many agents to choose from, the ones who get chosen offer something that the others did not. That is their value-added proposition. Learn to teach; teach to learn. Become a Master. Focus on consumer education.

CREATE YOUR PERFECT CUSTOMER

Residential real estate is first and foremost a business. It is a personal services business. Although your compensation may be generated by providing those services, that is not the business. Businesses are built from nothing, one step at a time. In a personal services business, you build your business one email address at a time.

The most common mistake made by new agents is failing to see real estate as a business. Consequently, they build nothing and start anew every day. Servicing someone else's low quality leads is not a business plan, it is a sure fire recipe for failure and gloom. Look at the movie *Glengarry Glen Ross*. You do not want to be dependent on someone else's leads; you want to build a referral water wheel where full buckets are continually coming up predisposed to select you.

Not everyone you meet will become a client and sign a contract with you, but almost everyone is in a position to refer a listing at some point. That referral will obviously have something in common with the person who recommended you.

In the world of business, the mention of a single name draws immediate respect — Peter Drucker. Drucker, who passed away in 2005 at the age of 97, is to business what Billy Graham is to religion, what Mozart is to music, and what DiMaggio is to baseball — a legend for the ages in his field of work.

For over 60 years, he influenced generations of business people as a teacher, writer, and business leader. He is widely regarded as the father of modern day management philosophy. His basic premise is more relevant to our business today than 50 years ago when he wrote, *The Practice of Management*, in which he raises the question of the very purpose of a business.

I often ask this question in my workshops, and overwhelmingly people agree that the purpose of a business is to make a profit. Drucker said they are wrong. This is the important lesson for us. Drucker said, *"There is only one valid definition of business purpose: **to create a customer**."* He noted that profit is the by-product of doing that well.

If you are waiting for customers to create themselves, "fuhgeddaboudit." They don't know how.

Drucker stressed this point:

"Markets are not created by God, nature, or economic forces, but by businessmen. The want they satisfy may have been felt by the customer before he was offered a means of satisfying it. There may have been no want at all until business action created it."

In this case, the want that you intend to create is the want of a trusted advisor. Who is sitting around wanting a real estate agent? Everyone already knows at least three and they probably do not like them. What people want is someone they can call when they confront complicated issues in life, even if they do not know you. I cannot tell you how many times my phone has rung and the caller said, "You don't know me, but a friend from work said you might be able to help us."

That is the sound of an incoming referral. But, it might have little or nothing to do with real estate. That could come later, or they could become a referral magnate. There are people out there who, if you do them a solid, will actively mine for listing referrals on your behalf. All you have to do is tell them about your business being dependent upon referrals and word of mouth.

TEN IMPORTANT IDEAS

If the purpose of a business is to create a customer, why not be selective? You will have virtually unlimited people to select from, so why not choose those among whom you can be most effective in generating referrals? Define your customer by personal characteristics, socio-economic status, employment, and recreation.

These are the people with whom you will be interacting. They will form your referral base so you must be able to relate to them and gain their absolute trust. I have rarely had an angry client because my perfect customer is kind, generous, thoughtful, understanding, intelligent, and possesses a great sense of humor. They were referred to me by people who possess the same qualities. My customer base comes largely from my recreational activities, so we tend to have something in common. Factors will depend on where you are, who your friends are, and where they live and work.

Some real estate practitioners are available 24/7 and will work with anyone. Those are two of the major causes of failure. Create a schedule and stick to it. You are methodically building a business, and that is the most important component of each and every day. Either schedule your time and run your own business, or strangers will run you right out of it.

Success is easy. Failure is miserable because failing out of real estate takes an economic toll, like a bad trip to the casino. There is an old joke that goes, "I got into real estate to sell, sell, sell … I've sold my house, my car, and my furniture … so far."

First of all, it is not selling; it is serving. Your only obstacle is that the entire universe of people does not have faith in your ability to capably address their issues. You have no street cred and no reputation.

Be honest, how many people do you know who see you as the person to turn to in a crisis? Let's see, there are you and your mom, your dingbat roommate from college, and maybe Nana, although she could probably go either way. That is the reputation you must build. You cannot do it overnight, but it can be done with careful planning and faithful execution.

Your only friend and your greatest enemy is your time. How you deploy this limited resource will determine how quickly you achieve the goals in your plan. You must set a weekly schedule and stick to it. Never eat lunch alone. Go to lunch with people who have nothing to do with real estate. Lunch is the arena where your game is won or lost. It could be over coffee or a cup of tea, but the sit-down, face to face, is where that other party becomes a potential source of referrals.

Though I believe in building a referral business through purposefully growing your relationship base, I also believe in selecting a geographic community and becoming an expert and the best-known real estate agent, no matter who got there before you.

Newer construction is ideal. Turnover begins within months, but tends to peak between year four and year 10 *(See Selecting the Community)*.

IDENTIFY AND DEVELOP YOUR UNIQUE SKILLS AND TALENTS

Everyone has unique skills and abilities. These are the keys to unlocking your full potential. They are also necessary to creating the perfect customers for you. No matter how hard you try, you can never be a better someone else; but if you do try, you can become a better you.

The No. 1 priority of a real estate business is meeting new people. That means get up, clean up, and show up every workday. If you meet one new person every day, five days a week, for the next five years, you will be earning a lot more than $50,000 per year.

How you meet them is just as important to the potential of your business. Do what you love to do and do it with others in a way that allows you to get to know the other participants. Everything from taking classes to participating in exercise programs provides great opportunities to cultivate relationships that lead to referrals.

People who share your interests generally share your values. Within their spheres of influence are more people who share your interests and values, and these will ultimately be your clients.

GET A MARKETABLE LISTING IN THE COMMUNITY THAT YOU WANT TO DOMINATE

Focus on listings. *Listings are hard to get.* They tend to go to agents with greater tenure in the business. They are generally the by-products of referrals. But, they are the foundation of your success in real estate.

Finding a listing will determine your future. You want listings, and the first one is the hardest. Markets come and go but, in most states, listings involve a contractual obligation to pay a fee when the listing sells within the term specified in the agreement.

Unqualified buyers are easy to get. Therefore, newer agents tend to spend a great deal of time trying to find ways to help unqualified buyers. But, unless you are contracting with the buyer (still not the norm in most states) they are free to shop around with anyone.

No one ever left the real estate business with a portfolio of salable listings. Yet throughout the ups and downs of more than three decades, I have often heard agents grumble that they were only going to work with buyers. Fatal error! Being dependent on buyers is like starting over every day with little to show for past efforts. Even worse, buyers are unreliable and targeting them, in particular first-time buyers, is a very poor business decision, as you will see.

The single most important goal of your real estate business is to build an inventory of salable listings. If you have listings, you have a contractual relationship to receive compensation. And, if you have done your job and properly priced the property, there is nothing you can do to prevent it from selling. Get the price right and you will be getting paid.

In many regions in the country, buyer/broker agreements are still more the exception than the norm. As a result, agents are sometimes reluctant to ask a buyer to enter into a binding agreement because they fear losing the buyer to an agent who does not require an agreement. Serving buyers is not as certain as representing sellers.

There is an extremely limited supply of real estate and a correspondingly high demand. There are lots of unqualified buyers willing to spend all of your time hoping you can find them a miracle. Listings are your security. Build and maintain an inventory of five to 10 listings and you will never worry about money again.

Listings create marketing opportunities, attract other listings, and sell whether you are working or on vacation. Your signs bring calls and produce higher quality buyers who have already seen the neighborhood and the exterior of the property.

Everyone wants to own real estate, so, by listing property you will have your pick of the most qualified buyers. Ask everyone you encounter, "Who do you know who might be thinking about selling their home?" It's as easy as that!

UNDERSTAND WHERE OPPORTUNITY COMES FROM

No matter how hard you work, your activities will not create sellers or buyers. Your objective is to channel them to you when they are ready. This is why the focus must be on building a referral network in which you are the trusted advisor.

Residential real estate activity is driven by predictable events that occur along life's continuum. Family formation, births, promotions, job transfers, reversal of fortune, job loss, illness, accident, divorce, and death are among the chief reasons why someone might need to consult with a knowledgeable real estate practitioner.

Well before any listing agreement is signed, people seek information regarding their options, the selling process, the market, net proceeds, and tax implications. If you have developed a referral business, you have now positioned yourself to be the one to provide an "initial consultation." This early access offers an unparalleled marketing advantage over most agents who are trying to connect with a buyer or seller who is "ripe." Later, these agents lose interest after two to three weeks of client inactivity. The trusted advisor, on the other hand, is there for the long haul. Once you understand the consumer's timetable, you will understand how this role is better suited to their needs.

A report on homebuyers and sellers by Hebert Research deserves a closer look for what it tells us about our potential clients. For example, buyers and sellers often take up to **four years** "collecting experiences" related to their current home and potential future needs.

After the "experience collecting phase," buyers spent **16.7 months**, on average, to research and buy their next home, but first-time buyers spent a whopping **20.5 months**. They take longer to mature than the average agent will be in business. Forty-four percent of buyers take **more than six months** "thinking" about desirable homes and neighborhoods before actually searching for listings. The average buyer then spends more than four months searching for homes. Once the research phase has been initiated, buyers spend an average of **7.1 months** in the "pre-research phase," **5.5 months** in the "active research phase," and **4.1 months** in the "active buying phase." The National Association of Realtors announced recently that the number of first-time buyers had decreased to 33 percent of all buyers. Correspondingly, they represent 0 percent of all listings.

Outside of the fact that all new and many experienced agents are targeting first-time buyers, they generally represent the greatest amount of work for the least amount of compensation.

Sellers, once they pass the experience collecting phase, take far less time moving through the phases. Sellers also spent up to four years subconsciously "collecting experiences." These experiences compound to bring the home sale to the forefront of consciousness, triggering a move to the "pre-research phase."

Once the research phase has been initiated, it takes sellers an average of **9.3 months** from the time they begin researching until they sell: **5.5 months** in the "pre-research phase," **1.4 months** for the "active research phase," and **2.4 months** for the "active selling phase."

Obviously, you will be meeting people in all phases, and a wise businessperson wants to know conclusively where the client fits into the process. First, because they cannot be rushed, and secondly, because you want to provide the level of service appropriate to their phase.

It could be that the phases are protracted because the clients are not receiving service appropriate to their phase. Around 80 percent of homebuyers start out seeking information on the internet, but there is so much content and distracting clutter that without experience to filter what is valid, it is not much help.

So, here is the key. According to the NAR, sellers list with the first agent they meet an extraordinary 73 percent of the time. A HouseValues Inc. study found 52.1 percent take only one day to select an agent. Buyers, on the other hand, spent up to three days rejecting candidates before selecting an agent. And why, according to HouseValues Inc., did consumers select the agents they did? Just as you might have guessed, they were chosen because of experience, honesty, and past relationships. They were already trusted advisors. And what did consumers want? They wanted someone to handle the paperwork and legal issues, who could negotiate on their behalf, and had access to listings.

SELECT THE RIGHT COMMUNITY

The main thrust of your business should be in building a referral business, but you still need to be an expert in available inventory and prices. Becoming an expert in a particular community or subdivision will make it easier to understand the entire marketplace.

Select a community near where you live so you can easily spend time there and be able to relate to the residents. Do not be tempted to choose a community just because you like it or the homes. That would be a plus, but this is a business decision and should be based on the people who live there.

Do not be deterred by first-time buyer homes; they have a rapid turnover rate and someone is always looking to buy the cheapest thing around, including investors. Here again, it is about the people who live there. They have never sold a home before and they need you. Move-up opportunities turn your listers into buyers, and vice versa. Real estate is one place where starting at the bottom can be the best opportunity.

There may be some temptation to target wealthy communities with the assumption that if you only close a handful of transactions, you will still get rich. You had better live there or be extremely close to someone who does, because the higher the price range, the greater the reliance on reputation and referrals in order to do business. You cannot just roll up to the clubhouse in your 1998 Honda Accord.

Go where your friends live. You want to be in an active community. You would like my neighborhood and my home, but you would starve to death due to the lack of turnover. Listings are rare, and the homes stay in the families for generations.

Newer construction provides a great door opener for you

"Hi, I'm Ben Selling from Super Realty. I'm trying to locate any of the original marketing materials from when the neighborhood was new. I like to use them with buyers, as well as in my listing marketing. You wouldn't happen to have anything like that, would you?"

Just because your community does not have new construction does not make this a bad idea. I got the new home brochure on a 25-year-old subdivision showing the original prices from an original homeowner. I made copies and left one at every house without further explanation. The phone rang off the hook as bewildered people called about the prices. A couple of callers were actually angry, but it was well worth it.

EXPLOIT THE OPEN HOUSE OPPORTUNITY

An open house is a legal excuse to plaster the neighborhood with your name.

While luck and signage will bring buyers to the home, your

real goal of obtaining future listings requires that you send the right message to residents who will be sellers in the future. This is your showcase. You want it to look, feel and smell great. Fresh paint, spruced up landscaping, clean windows, and no clutter are important evidence of what kind of advice you give sellers. Look for a home that is located near well-traveled streets.

The success of your open house should not be measured by how many possible buyers you picked up; rather the success of your open house should be measured according to the neighbors you have made a positive impression upon. Think of it as a low-key block party — you want the neighbors to stop in. *(See Chapter 10: Open House with a Purpose).*

GUARD YOUR REPUTATION

It takes years to build a reputation and seconds to destroy it. Because your business is dependent upon you being recommended by others, your reputation is your most important asset. As you can see from the statistics above, it takes time to build and market that reputation. You cannot undo the damage.

How does the public perceive real estate agents in general? It is not very favorable. Being on the frontlines as long as I have, I have met a lot of real estate agents who are unreliable, irresponsible, dishonest, ignorant, and nasty. Do not be that person.

Do not focus on the money. Focus on growth — personal growth and business growth. Living that philosophy every day will attract all that you need. You may never be wealthy, but the kind of income security you can build from focusing on building a referral business will be worth it.

ACHIEVE YOUR FULL POTENTIAL DOING THINGS YOU ENJOY

If you can shift your paradigm from real estate sales to personal growth and development, you will attract all that you need. Real estate is a wonderful arena in which to grow and discover oneself while pursuing rewarding activities.

What you truly enjoy says a lot about who you are; you cannot be someone you are not. You cannot do what anyone else does and no one can do what you can do. How and where you meet people and make friends is not nearly as important as how much fun you have doing it.

Several years ago a woman stopped me at this point in my presentation and objected strenuously on the grounds that she did not believe in mixing business with pleasure and she would never be comfortable doing business with friends. I said, "I believe in mixing pleasure with everything and my business activities have produced a lot of good friends."

I am not saying that you cannot succeed digging for ripe strangers, but why would you want to? The very reason that people do not prospect is that they find it unpleasant. Picture this in your mind. You have learned all that there is to learn about the details of your craft, and as a result, you are relaxed as you sit down with people who have heard good things about you.

For 30 years, I made a living playing softball. Softball players buy and sell houses, but more importantly, so do their friends, families, co-workers, neighbors, parents, and children. If you played on my team, a listing referral would get you the best bat or glove that money could buy and every player knew it. You cannot pay a referral fee to an unlicensed individual but you can give reasonable tokens of appreciation. When you are a young man with a family, a new $300 bat is not much of an option.

Make a list of 10 things you enjoy doing and see how many have people-meeting potential. If none of them do, real estate is probably not the best career choice for your disposition.

Be yourself, but be an ever improving you. Real estate is a "Top Producer" culture where "coffee is for closers." Almost every company has some type of award or recognition program that gives plaques or trophies for categories such as "Most Listings Taken," "Most Listings Closed," "Most Sales," and "Most Money Earned."

This fosters a false competition over the wrong things, resulting in attempting to match, copy, or exceed someone else. This distracts focus from what is more important than anything, the establishment and accomplishment of individual goals and objectives that produce the level of results that you want, not artificial and predetermined categories. The very point of building a referral business is to avoid competition and build something unique to you with your uniqueness as the value-added-proposition. Be yourself, everyone else is already taken. To paraphrase Walt Disney, the most valuable asset you possess is your uniqueness.

TECHNOLOGY AND SOCIAL MEDIA WILL NOT SAVE YOU

Real estate as a profession was a reluctant participant in the expansion of business technology, and as a result, many outside entities saw opportunity to capture the data created by agents for a multiple listing service and sell them the leads that could be mined from that system.

But, technology is just a toolbox, and the tools are made for specific purposes. The primary activities of your business are meeting people, creating a highly favorable impression, actively pursuing listing referrals, giving great service, and growing yourself to grow your business.

Database (Community)

Your database *is* your business. The people you know and the people you intend to meet will be collected here. Growing the size and improving the quality of that database are the two most important things you will do each and every day. Have a backup.

Simple daily goals such as meet one new person, contact five people you already know, set one firm appointment for the future, and have one face-to-face meeting with someone you know about the importance of referrals will improve your short term odds of survival while building a business for a lifetime. That is the real estate business. Do something you enjoy doing, do it with others, select those who meet your criteria, add them to your database, ask for referrals, deliver top quality service, and repeat again tomorrow.

Website

Your website is like a meeting place for your database if you use it properly. I have looked at hundreds of agent websites and most of them do a disservice to the agent. With so many company provided templates, I am surprised agents are not doing more.

Social media can be a terrific tool, but what messages are you sending? Are they important enough to break through the clutter of social media?

CHAPTER 3

THE ETHICAL BUSINESS MODEL

"If you tell the truth, you don't have to remember anything."
—MARK TWAIN

It has seemed to me that the real estate industry has always viewed ethics as a sort of impediment to doing business. In fact, the National Association of Real Estate requires its members to complete a course in ethics. Yet, at the same time, it fosters an environment of such steep competition that temptation is everywhere. Embracing ethical business practices requires rethinking our entire approach to the business.

THE ACTIVITY - FROM PROSPECTING TO SELECTING

Prospecting, by definition, implies looking hard for something there is not much of. It is anybody, anywhere, anytime. Your broker does not care who your clients turn out to be, but you should. Once you determine who your ideal client is, you will be able to create a plan to attract them to you. By selecting rather than prospecting, you improve your chances of generating listing referrals. Stop pursuing business; instead, start to create business.

THE OBJECTIVE - FROM LEAD GENERATION TO REFERRAL CREATION

Lead generating comes from the idea that you should be looking for "*deals*" to do. It is a process of sifting through people looking for a *"ripe one."* Focusing on getting a deal on the board may be good for your broker, but is not so good for building your business.

Referral creation requires a one-on-one, face-to-face, sit-down meeting with everyone you know for the purpose of gaining their support, trust, and desire to help you build your business by referring members of their sphere (community) to you. It has nothing to do with getting their *"deal."*

THE ARENA – FROM GEOGRAPHY TO COMMUNITY

When I began my real estate career, I was given a section of the local map containing about 500 homes and armloads of my broker's door-hangers with the admonishment that if I did not farm my area, it would be given to another agent. It was a sweaty June afternoon, about six months later, when the notion crossed my mind that, from my broker's perspective, I was cheaper than postage.

But, I was not getting any listings this way and I sure was not having any fun. I was definitely open to new ideas when I came across a study done by Watkins Company, who used to sell spices and household items door-to-door. They found that 70 percent of American homes no longer had an adult decision maker at home during the day. Conclusion: I had been spending my time in the wrong place.

When I mentioned it to my broker, he handed me the reverse directory and told me to start calling them at night. This was not fun either and proved no more productive.

Talk about the teacher appearing when the student is ready. It was a Real Estate Today profile of three successful agents and each said the same thing. They all attributed their business to a steady stream of referrals.

THE ETHICAL BUSINESS MODEL

In that instant I realized what no one in the trenches around me had realized; the world had changed, but the industry had not. The geographic approach to the business was the by-product of the days of Sinclair Lewis' fictional real estate broker of the 1920s, George F. Babbitt.

The widespread adoption of both the automobile and the telephone was just beginning in 1920. The effective message of a real estate broker did not extend more than a few blocks beyond his office. There was no choice but to employ geographic advertising. The technology of today, however, allows your message to go wherever it might be best received.

The neighborhood has been replaced by communities rooted in affinity rather than geography. You may not know your neighbor, but you could know Kevin Bacon. Your community is made up of everyone you know. Maybe 50 to 500 people, including Kevin, with whom you interact in the course of going about your life.

As you build and improve your business, you should never lose sight of the need to constantly add new people to your community; to increase your referrals or improve their quality.

Whether you call it your sphere of influence, network, database, friends and family, or community, it is an intertwining of people who come together largely for mutual benefit or out of necessity and often have each other's well-being in mind. The people who currently populate your community will change as you select new members and delete others and as normal attrition takes its toll. Therefore, every day that you tell yourself you *worked* in real estate should include the conscious, scheduled act of selecting one new member of your community. In a year, that is 250 people that you selected based not on the likelihood of getting their "*deal*," but upon the probability that they would refer your perfect customer to you.

Make no mistake, the names, email addresses, street addresses and phone numbers of the people in your community comprise the primary asset of your business. Their receptiveness to your message is the key to your success, so choose well. As you build and improve your business, you should never lose sight of the need to constantly add new people to your community, either for the purpose of increasing your referrals or for improving their quality.

THE ROLE – FROM SALESPERSON TO TRUSTED ADVISOR

In addition to changing the arena, you will need to change the role that you play. No longer should you pay the obsequious lackey trolling the neighborhood hungry for a "*deal*." There are enough of those already.

What consumers want to find is a competent, knowledgeable professional who is neither an egomaniac, dumb as a stump, nor a certified head case. Enter you, well groomed, well-mannered, patient, empathetic, and professionally curious as to whether you can be of assistance. You are neither "*deal*" hungry nor in any particular hurry. Your mission is to be certain that a potential client is fully aware of all of their options and what the possible implications of each might be. Your new role is that of "trusted advisor."

THE RELATIONSHIP – FROM FUNCTIONARY TO FIDUCIARY

Functionaries put up signs, hang lock boxes, and find available property. Fiduciaries are purveyors of expertise and trust.

THE SERVICE – FROM SELLING TO COUNSELING

Your service is your counseling. If you can explain it well enough so that the benefits are apparent to the client, no selling or closing is required. Selling is the act of going out and finding someone who can be persuaded to utilize your services.

The trusted advisor markets an image to a selected community for the purpose of generating a steady stream of referrals predisposed to use his or her services. It is an entirely different dynamic that produces an entirely different relationship with the client. Real estate is confusing, and consumers need counseling.

THE PACE – FROM YOUR TIMETABLE TO THE CLIENT'S TIMETABLE

The trusted advisor has a role to play well before any real estate activity occurs. This early access offers an unparalleled marketing advantage over most agents trying to connect with a buyer or seller that is *"ripe."* Later these agents lose interest after two to three weeks of client inactivity. But, the trusted advisor is there for the long haul. And, when you understand the consumer's timetable, you will understand how the role of adviser is better suited to his or her needs.

As noted earlier, a study commissioned by HouseValues Inc. revealed that homebuyers and sellers took anywhere from one to five years considering their options prior to finally making a move. A lot of salespeople will pass through the business during that time. But, it is during this period that the pre-existing trusted advisor is closing out the competition.

According to NAR research, 74 percent of sellers list with the first agent they meet. If you have been regularly providing information and fulfilling the role of trusted advisor, this agent will be you.

Listings come to market because of predictable life changes in the weeks and months surrounding those changes. It is in times of great upheaval and stress that people wonder who they can turn to for guidance. If you have positioned yourself properly, people will call you. Their calls will not always be about real estate, but be a good counselor anyway.

I see myself as a sort of Godfather-type character. People call me when they have problems because I have established myself as someone who "knows about these things." Build relationships with others and get things handled for those in your community; every now and then you will get a listing referral because you "know about these things."

THE PROCESS - FROM PROMOTION TO ATTRACTION

Salespeople are always promoting themselves. We see pictures of them with their kids, their cars, their cellphones, and their golf clubs, standing in front of "sold" signs and flaunting multiple million-dollar producer designations on their business cards.

In the words of Shania Twain, *"That don't impress me much."*

Trusted advisors attract their pick of high quality referrals through their character, competence and highly professional demeanor. This goes a long way toward explaining that, despite the logic of this approach, it is the road less traveled in this industry. Many simply do not possess the attributes to be anything other than salespeople.

THE ETHICAL BUSINESS MODEL

THE FOCUS - FROM FIRST-TIME BUYERS TO FIRST-TIME SELLERS

While I understand that first-time buyers make up a significant part of the market, I do not understand why every new agent gets all gooey about how much they like working with first-time buyers. Is it because new agents surmise that first-time buyers are the only people who know less than they do about real estate?

From the viewpoint of someone having been in the industry for 35 years, first-time buyers represent 0 percent of the listings sold, and listings are your lifeblood. First-time buyers are often worse than ill informed; they are often misinformed. They listen to everyone else, which makes them skittish. In terms of time spent for the return, they are the least profitable segment of the market.

On the other hand, first-time sellers usually do not know much about real estate either, and the agent who sold them the home has probably left the business. So there they are with a property to sell and no one to help them. Because the phrase "first-time seller" has yet to be coined, you have a heck of a jump on the market. Who needs a trusted advisor more than a first-time seller?

THE CHANGE - FROM EXTERNAL TO INTERNAL

When we are not getting the results we want, it is just common sense to ask, "what can be changed?" All too often we end up changing everything but the one thing that can make a difference and the only thing over which we have much influence — ourselves.

Becoming a trusted advisor requires constant personal growth and development. You must become the person people turn to in a crisis for advice and counsel. The ultimate goal is to build a better you.

THE GOAL - FROM MAKING MONEY TO ACHIEVING MASTERY

This brings us to the true goal — to achieve mastery through our profession. Nothing less will bring the rewards and satisfaction that you desire. Anything less is settling for less.

The problem is that there really are no shortcuts to mastery. In the beginning, you will earn what you are worth — nothing. So, the first step is acknowledging that you must build value in yourself to be able to attract people willing to pay large amounts of money to handle their needs. And, more importantly, you must attract people willing to refer you to their friends, relatives, neighbors, and co-workers.

People must be able to see the connection between the value you bring and the rewards you are getting. How are you adding value to the lives of others worthy of so much money? It had better be more than salesmanship. A recent NAR study found that both buyers and sellers placed the highest value on the reputation of the practitioner. All of those vague issues that seemed so remote and uninteresting back in license school really are the stock and trade of the true real estate professional. For $25,000, the client actually expects that you know what every one of those forms, disclosures, and contracts are all about. By mastering the competencies, we make ourselves more valuable.

For the master, deception is unnecessary; therefore, ethical behavior becomes the only option. You have an ethical duty to pursue mastery. You must be committed to rising to a higher calling and accept the time necessary to become one of an elite few who really know what they are doing. We must insist on

THE ETHICAL BUSINESS MODEL

earning our rewards and be committed to settling for nothing less than the satisfaction of a reward earned through effort, persistence, and sacrifice.

Remember my Mantor Mantra: *"I don't want something for nothing; I always find out later that I can't afford it."*

Your reputation is your most valuable business asset. Your reputation does not come from your advertising and marketing, it comes from what others say about you. Either create, nurture, and protect that reputation or you will never get any real traction in your business. It can take years to build and only seconds to destroy. Make ethical behavior a habit. When temptation comes along, you will be conditioned to resist. Build a model that attracts listing referrals. Counsel, do not persuade. Become more valuable. Be empathetic and always live the Golden Rule.

CHAPTER 4

THE BUSINESS PLAN

"The purpose of a business is to create a customer."
—PETER F. DRUCKER

Before the rubber meets the road, the driver must commit to a destination and a direction. Planning and implementing your business plan is as simple as setting out on a road trip, and yet, there seems to be a sort of natural resistance to the process. As a result, most real estate agents fritter away their valuable time aimlessly pursuing something that does not exist.

Over my years in the real estate business, I have interviewed hundreds of new licensees and experienced agents looking for a fresh start. I recall asking one about her earning expectations and she replied, "Oh, I'm not looking to get rich, I just want my fair share."

I said, "Your fair share is less than zero; you either have to create it or try to take it away from someone else."

The fundamental obstacle to building a rewarding real estate business is that there are too many agents chasing too few deals and that manifests itself in ways that are often unpleasant. The answer is obvious, do not be dependent upon getting your fair share of unclaimed business; create your own customers, as Drucker advises.

Businesses are built one brick at a time. One warm smile, one firm handshake and one random act of kindness at a time. But, how? That is what the business plan does; it gets us to "how."

The business plan needn't be elaborate or difficult. It is simply a means of answering a series of questions leading to the action steps that break down into your daily activities.

- What do I want?
- When do I want it?
- What needs to happen between now and then?
- What do I do first?
- When do I do it?
- How will I do it?
- How am I doing?

The worst plan, faithfully administered, is far more likely to succeed than no plan at all.

FIFTEEN SIMPLE STEPS: WHAT TO DO, HOW TO DO IT, AND WHY

This business plan will provide you with the direction and the tools you will need to build a financially rewarding and personally fulfilling referral business. Do not be misled by those diehard sales dinosaurs; you can get a referral today.

Visualize everyone you know standing side-by-side, holding hands, and behind them everyone they know. The people behind them will have real estate needs whether you do anything about it or not. Your job is to influence the thinking of the people you know and will meet, such that they become proactive on your behalf. The people you know can lead you directly to everyone they know that has a real estate-related issue, or they can prevent you from knowing about it by simply doing nothing.

If you create a plan and follow it, you will build a steady stream of high quality referrals predisposed to utilize wonderful you. You will also uncover any immediate business just as effectively as lead generating, prospecting, and closing sales dinosaurs.

The key is to have enough people enthusiastic about you to refer substantial business. It is word of mouth with a mission. It is about developing a reputation for excellence. You either set out to build that reputation or you are relegated to the road of cheesy closes and awkward tie-downs, doing deals and closing leads. The goals you set, the customer you strive to create, and the methods you use will either contribute to or detract from your likelihood of success. Plan well.

A business plan seeks to answer three fundamental questions: "What do I want?" "When do I want it?" and "What has to happen between now and then?"

It should not be viewed as some mind-numbing, number crunching exercise, but more like an autobiography to be reviewed and revised as you continue to see the power of living life by design. The only limitation to what you can achieve in a personal service business is your imagination and your commitment to implementing the daily little pieces that build the foundation.

1. Get a clear focus

Your immediate survival and your long-term success in any personal service business, from the practice of law to acrylic wraps, and from dentistry to dog grooming, is dependent on you succeeding in generating a sufficient number of targeted customers. You must commit regular time and energy to creating future customers that are ever more profitable to serve.

Despite the seeming wisdom of hanging out a shingle and advertising in the local newspaper, you will not create many customers that way because they do not need you at the moment, and there is too much clutter for your individual message to break through.

THE BUSINESS PLAN

Most advertising is intended to trigger an immediate response. Go to Macy's; buy the sweater. That is why it is largely understood by industry management that real estate advertising can affect the company's brand awareness, but does not create many customers. What it does accomplish is attracting agents that mistakenly believe the company will create good customers for them.

No customer exists until you create him or her. So, why not improve your chances for long-term success by rejecting the notion of "any client, anywhere, anytime" in favor of attracting the perfect client for you. My perfect client is intelligent, curious, patient, optimistic, honest, empathetic, interesting, flexible, and fun. I believe that my satisfaction from what I do comes from the people I associate with. Choose well.

2. Evaluate the marketplace

Traditional prospecting and lead generating activities are largely out of sync with the way and manner in which real estate comes to the marketplace. Never lose sight of your ultimate target —the listings of first-time sellers. With so much of the industry targeting first-time buyers, it is just good business to create listings. The faster you build a base of marketable listings, the more likely you are to survive.

First-time home sellers tend to be concentrated in entry-level neighborhoods. Unlike the custom homes scattered along the tree-shaded hillsides where owners stay for 30 years, many of these owners are anxious to move up. They are just waiting for you to show them how. These are the most affordable homes in a community and have a much higher turnover rate. Plus, they provide the opportunity to earn additional brokerage fees by placing the loan and facilitating the replacement transaction.

Listings are rarely the result of a perfectly timed cold call. They are not the by-product of a capricious decision induced by a smooth talking salesperson or an advertising campaign. Real estate listings are the natural consequence of a handful of predictable life events. Marriage, birth of a child, career advancement, job transfer, retirement, divorce, injury, illness, aging, and death carry with them vitally important decisions and forward planning regarding real estate. Remember that the Hebert Research study revealed that buyers and sellers of real estate enter into a protracted decision-making process that runs from several months to several years.

It is often in times of family confusion and despair that people most need an empathetic, well-informed, competent, trusted advisor. Any salesperson can get a listing under these circumstances, but only a trusted advisor would advise against selling an appreciating asset if there were other alternatives. Nobody in real estate ever got an award for declining a listing, but trusted advisors frequently pass up easy money in favor of increasing their professional value.

Remember that the NAR study showed that 74 percent of home sellers listed with the first and only agent they spoke with, suggesting that the agent was not being plucked from the Yellow Pages at the last minute but was very likely part of an ongoing deliberation regarding future real estate needs. Your purpose is to be your clients' trusted advisor while they are considering the impact of these life events. You do not want to be in the position of competing with other agents days before the decision.

3. *Analyze the competition*

What the competition lacks in real advantage it makes up for in sheer numbers. That fact alone deserves special attention. How many agents are there in your region? What do they do to create customers? What products and services do they provide? How can you displace them?

THE BUSINESS PLAN

Over the last few years, I have heard the emergence of the phrase, "I do real estate" to describe one's occupational status. Try this instead: *"I assist my clients in utilizing other people's money to acquire appreciating assets on which the profits can be 100 percent tax free; is that something you would be interested in hearing more about?"*

In an instant you have changed the game, and if you have changed the game, you have gained the advantage and crippled the competition. Your perfect customer will be completely immune to their message. Your customers will respond more favorably to the ongoing message of leverage, utility, and tax-free profits than an actor pretending to be a real estate agent dancing on a dining room table.

Most of the real estate industry is looking for a qualified buyer to sell a house to and right now. You want listings. You will get buyers along the way.

4. Set realistic, specific and measurable goals, objectives, milestones and targets

My experience trying to help people set goals can be summed up this way: most people do not know what they want, but they are pretty sure they do not have it.

There is something so seductive about the comfort zone that embraces us in the 21st century that it can be hard to want more than another burger and a sit-com. If you cannot find a connection between the risk, routine activities, long hours, and what you really want, you will be back in front of the big screen with a Big Mac and a tiny future in real estate.

The absolute need for cash might make you a more aggressive salesperson, but it won't do much to help you build a business. That has to be tied to more than money. You have to be absolutely clear about what you value, and that can take a little painful soul searching. I get the feeling that some people will not set goals because they do not want to place any limitations on themselves. The reality is that you cannot do everything, have everything, or be everything, so choosing is vital to getting what really matters to you.

One thing is for certain, you will need to earn money to pay your bills and provide for the things that you want in your future. Not all goals are monetary, but those that have a monetary component need to be reflected in your budget so that your business plan incorporates the appropriate amount of activity necessary to achieve them. With an effective plan, you can either increase the number of referrals you create or increase your profitability.

Goals are the big picture motivators. An example would be earning the amount of money your budget calls for.

Objectives are the things you must achieve to attain the goal, such as taking 35 marketable listings per year.

Milestones are the exercises that lead to attaining the objectives. There is a direct relationship between doing CMAs (Comparative Market Analysis) and obtaining listings. A milestone might be to present two CMAs per week.

Targets are those manageable little daily activities that lead to the milestones. Schedule the time and place to meet one new person per day. Schedule one sit-down, face-to-face referral dialogue with a member of your community. Commit to ending every conversation with a Columbo-like, *"Oh, by the way, who do you know that might be thinking about selling their house?"* Those are targets within your control.

5. *Define your market*

Every year, seven out of 100 homeowners sell their homes. If you market to 100 people, it is highly unlikely that you will be 100 percent effective in listing all of their homes and selling them. In fact, you probably won't earn enough to afford the median priced home in your area.

But, if your true objective was the listings of the family, friends, neighbors, co-workers, and acquaintances of those people, your market is a community of 10,000 who will combine to sell 700 homes every year. If you fail to capture 95 percent, you will still generate 35 listings. Market effectively to 200 people or more as a way of increasing the number of referrals you receive and being more selective. Your marketplace is the combined spheres of influence of every individual for whom you have a name, address, and phone number. The foundation of your business will be the relationships you create.

The real estate business is not an endless sea of houses that have to be sold to unwitting buyers. It should be about helping our community take advantage of the extraordinary benefits of leverage, utility, and tax-free profits associated with planned real estate ownership. The role of trusted advisor emphasizes the fiduciary duties of the business over the more functionary duties.

Real estate is a highly complex and legal arena impacted in one way or another by numerous regulations emanating from all governments. Choosing the role of salesperson does not relieve you of your responsibility for knowing what will take years to master. These are the stock in trade of the trusted advisor. You cannot fake competence.

6. *Develop your strategy*

Meet people, make friends, ask for referrals, give service, and ask for referrals.

That is it. I wish there were more to it than that. Every true workday must have a scheduled time and place to meet a new person. Every workday should consist of an appointment with someone in your community for the purpose of obtaining their enthusiastic commitment to help you grow your business

The best places to meet people who are likely to be good referral sources for you are the places you like to go to in order to do the things you like to do. People who share the same interests and passions often share a sense of camaraderie. The wonderful thing about a personal service business is that your No. 1 objective is to meet people that will rave about you to everyone they know. You can do that anywhere you like. In my case, I like to play softball. Softball players have jobs, families, friends, and neighbors; those people may even come to the games. One of my associates is a top pool player. His clients are like the characters in a Damon Runyon novel; but, that too is worth noting. You catch what you fish for.

The possibilities are endless — from evening classes on your favorite topics, to a local hot rod club; from community involvement, to a book club. Do what you love to do and you will attract the best referral sources and, by extension, the best customers for you. You are growing your community, so you might as well populate it with like-minded individuals.

7. Create your marketing plan

The word "marketing" is used frequently, but is rarely defined and is the source of much confusion. Marketing is taking control of a piece of a person's mind. If you manufacture toothpaste, you market nationwide. If you have a personal service business, you market within your community. That is an advantage.

Products like Colgate® and Tide® are leaders in their product categories and represent effective marketing. As products, they are not markedly different from all of the others in their

THE BUSINESS PLAN

category, yet the consumer voluntarily selects those brands without regard to pricing. When it comes to toothpaste and laundry soap, these brands have taken a piece of the consumer's mind and positioned themselves as No. 1.

Your goal is to take and hold the No. 1 position in the minds of at least 200 selected individuals such that any time those individuals think about real estate or home loans, your image pops into their mind. You probably already hold the No. 1 position in the minds of those closest to you, such as relatives and friends. You want to add someone to that group every day. If you work 250 days per year, you are building a good-sized community, or at least improving its quality.

It is all about positioning. If you cannot immediately get the No. 1 position, take the No. 2 position and be consistent. Eventually, that No. 1 position will come open and you will fill it quite nicely.

Everything you need to influence the thinking of a few hundred people is readily available to you. Treat those few hundred people all as potential real estate investors and teach them about the benefits of planned real estate ownership. Send them real estate information and tell them what it means to them. Invite them to workshops where they can learn the pillars of real estate investing and how to do it. Most consumers do not know what is possible; they will be grateful to you for enlightening them and will sing lofty praises of you to all who will listen. Even better, if you go the extra mile, when people tell them about their lives, they will recommend you as a person to talk to. Not a real estate salesperson, but someone to talk to — a trusted advisor.

Develop your brand to further distinguish yourself from the rest of the herd. Seek professional design help; you will be stuck with the results for a long time.

8. Schedule the implementation of the plan

Time slips away. It is easy to get caught up in real estate activities, but being busy does not equate to being effective. Did you work today? Did you add a new person to your community? Did you have a sit-down, face-to-face referral dialogue?

For these things to occur, they must actually be scheduled as appointments. Time management will be critical to maintaining any balance and keeping you on course.

9. Launch the plan

Now go out and do it! You must go out and talk to people about your business. What you talk about should be aligned with your strategy. You want to raise their antennas so that they are alert to circumstances that lead them to refer you.

10. Review, analyze, re-launch

What gets measured gets done. As a business person, you must put in place a measure of accountability. Many large corporations review their progress annually and revise their plans accordingly. You have an advantage in that you can review your progress weekly and have 52 opportunities to correct course.

I created the Red Zone Time Planning System to use as a daily planner and a business review. It helps track the important growth areas of your business, such as number of people in your community, the number of referral dialogues conducted, and the growth in the dollar value of your business. It also serves as a reminder that there are many areas that need to be planned and scheduled in order to create the business of your dreams and plans.

11. Differentiate

If you are doing what everyone else is doing, you will get the results they are getting — another career adjustment. You need to distance yourself from the herd of look alike, talk alike salespeople.

Find a niche, or a couple of niches; learn everything that can be known about those niches, and selectively market to their members.

12. Develop your brand

By developing your own brand and image, you can position yourself ahead of any company image. People relate to other people more than they do brands and totems.

13. Build a database

By utilizing modern communications technology, you have the ability to influence the thinking of hundreds of people or more. You do not need to advertise to the whole world, just to 100-500 people that you select.

14. Implement systems to ensure consistency

Once your database is in place, routine marketing and follow-up can be systematized to allow you to spend more time with clients.

15. Submit to coaching/consulting

To move beyond your current performance, you will have to adopt a new way of thinking and perfect certain disciplines. This can only be done with the help of a coach or consultant.

The masters of any endeavor invariably have a coach. NFL Pro Bowl quarterback Drew Brees has several specialized coaches who work with him on individual aspects of his performance including biomechanical efficiency, vision, optimum nutrition, and strategic thinking. The point of coaching is to help an individual attain their personal best. The competition in the NFL is so great, like real estate, that committed players want to leave nothing to chance and are always seeking that slight edge. Coaching provides that edge.

Starting out brand new in the real estate business is risky. Many are called; few are chosen to earn a living. But, if you do everything you can think of to succeed, you will never have to look back and wonder what might have been.

CHAPTER 5

SELECTING THE RIGHT BROKER

"Management is about arranging and telling. Leadership is about nurturing and enhancing."
—TOM PETERS

You are unique and so too will be your business. If you intend to develop an ethics based referral business, you will want to associate with a firm that shares and will nurture those values.

IDENTITY

New licensees frequently select their broker based on the amount of advertising they do. The rationale being that all of that advertising ought to produce some "*deals*" for me, since, although no one knows who *I* am, they will have confidence in the brand of my broker.

The broker really is not advertising to attract business for you. If advertising generated a large number of perspective buyers and sellers, you would be working for a small salary rather than a large percentage.

The broker's purpose in advertising is to advance the strength of the corporate brand and to attract a continuous pool of new licensees to replace last year's crop who have done their handful of "*deals*" and are going back to work, possibly at their old jobs.

For you to distinguish yourself from the pack of salespeople, you will need a brand of your own. It could be just your name if it is distinctive. Who could forget a name like Octavius Hoehandle or Freckles Schwartz? But, if you were not fortunate enough to be born with a memorable or unique name, you can always make one up. Nobody crowned Mike Cerrone the Condo King; he just seized a marketing advantage. At the same time, he seized a niche and conveys it through his brand. It does not prevent him from representing any client, but it does give him a solid foothold in the minds of his community.

As a new licensee, you will need to contract with a broker in order to conduct business. Beyond that requirement, you may need other things from your broker. There are bare minimum brokerage services with no offices and little else that charge either a transaction fee or a monthly fee. Few people are equipped to go it alone right from the beginning.

The first consideration is location. I did not create my offices with the idea of sheltering real estate agents from contact with the public. I created the office to be a resource to enhance their credibility. With so many agents seemingly working out of the trunks of their cars, it can be a market advantage to meet clients in a professional environment that conveys an image of stability, especially when you have no reputation to fall back on.

As much as possible, try to arrange an initial consultation with any potential client in your office. It is safe, and resources are available. Many agents meet new buyers in the office, but few meet sellers there, choosing instead to go right to their homes. That may be the best way in some cases, but I find that presenting market information has more credibility when produced and presented in a business environment rather than the kitchen table.

Never forget that if you fail to price the property at market value, it will not be seen by the right buyers. As a listing agent,

SELECTING THE RIGHT BROKER

you will only have influence over the seller. Get the listing price right, and you will be closing soon. In most cases, there will be a sizable gap between the seller's expectation and true market value. I believe that delivering this news is best accomplished in a professional office rather than a dinner table.

In addition to a place to meet clients, you want to know who will be answering the 1,001 questions you will have in your first couple of years. Will you have a coach in-house? Will you be mentored out to a seasoned agent and split your compensation with them?

Your choices are large national brands, franchise brands, regional independents, and single local offices. Will the name of the company matter? No. The entire purpose of your business is to enhance your brand image as the go-to person in real estate, not them. If their brands attracted real clients, they would not turn them over to you. Further, and more importantly, despite their size and brand, their agents fare no better than anyone else's, and many times they actually do worse.

Here is how I would evaluate a potential office:

1. Is it easy to get to with little direction?
2. Is signage appropriate?
3. Is there ample parking?
4. Is the exterior well maintained?
5. Does it feel safe? Is it well lit?
6. Can I see where I want to go?
7. When I enter the interior of the office does it look neat, clean, well maintained, and cheerful?
8. What is the vibe? Is there activity and enthusiasm? Do the people seem friendly and helpful?
9. Where is the leadership coming from?
10. Does leadership inspire confidence?
11. What is their reputation and background?

WHAT TO LOOK FOR IN A BROKERAGE

The first and most important decision you will make is to select the right brokerage. There are many things to consider when evaluating a brokerage, but here are six important elements to examine when choosing a broker affiliation.

1. Stability

A lot of offices have closed, scattering experienced and new agents in search of new accommodations. The last thing you want when you are just starting out is to be forced to start over at a new brokerage.

2. Reputation

Let's face it. Coming into the business as a new agent, your reputation, to the extent that you have one, will be for being inexperienced. No matter how much your friends like and trust you, they might be uncomfortable appointing you the agent for a rather sizable transaction. While you cannot immediately overcome the stigma of being new, you can diminish the apprehension of potential clients by associating with a brokerage that has a strong local reputation.

3. Training

Learning the real estate business is like a long, slow walk down a country road. There are no shortcuts, and hurrying will not help; the destination is the journey. Training is the difference between going on the journey with a seasoned guide to point out the things that lack of experience might obscure and going it alone. Training is a process, not an event, so it should be ongoing, regular, varied, and relevant to the needs of the individual at different career levels.

4. Location

There are many aspects to location. Because you will be leveraging your brand by co-branding with the broker, you will want your potential clients to have the brand reinforced through repetition. Is there signage that can be seen by residents going in and out of the community? Is the location convenient, and are there other services nearby? Is there ample and easily accessible parking nearby so clients are not stressed and cranky when they arrive?

5. Experienced leadership

Real estate companies come and go in sync with the rise and fall of the volume of business. You want to associate with someone who has been through the challenges, as well as the easy money. A broker cannot teach what they do not know.

6. Listings

From the time that you actually announce your entry into the real estate business until your marketing efforts begin to produce results, you will be dependent upon "leads." Your long-term goal is to generate referrals from the people in your database, but until that begins to happen, you will have to sift through a lot of warm bodies hoping to find something that might result in earning a fee. A well-located office with a substantial number of listings could provide the opportunity to hold open houses and to meet walk-in or phone-in prospects.

"People are always blaming their circumstances for what they are. I don't believe in circumstances. The people who get on this world are the ones who get up and look for the circumstances they want, and if they can't find them, make them."
—GEORGE BERNARD SHAW, *MRS. WARREN'S PROFESSION*

CHAPTER 6

EFFECTIVE COMMUNICATION IS YOUR BUSINESS

"What we've got here is a failure to communicate. Some men you just can't reach,"
—STROTHER MARTIN,
AS THE WARDEN IN *COOL HAND LUKE*.

Failure to communicate is a fact of everyday life. How often do we hear, "Nobody told me," "I couldn't open my email," or "I didn't get the message"?

THE IMPORTANCE OF CLEAR COMMUNICATION

Success in business is largely dependent upon our ability to transmit our message. What we say, how we say it, and the media we employ are critical to effective communication. Others rely on us to collect, process, and distribute vital information competently and in a timely manner. We set appointments and reschedule them. We make representations and commitments. We interpret laws, codes, and rules. We are responsible for millions of dollars changing hands based on representations we make.

If you have a failure to communicate in business, you could lose a client, lose a friend, lose a transaction, lose a suit, lose your license, or maybe even lose your freedom. It can happen so easily because we tend to take for granted that we are good communicators when, in fact, most of us know very little about effective communication.

EFFECTIVE COMMUNICATION IS YOUR BUSINESS

I was lost in thought when the ringing of the phone shattered my concentration. Not wanting to get derailed from what I was working on, I decided to let voicemail take care of it. Though it turned out to be a wrong number, I had to pick it up. It was a government agency and the message was intended for a prospective grant recipient. The caller warned that she had 48 hours to respond to his call, and no other attempt would be made to contact her.

Had the intended recipient been "The Amazing Kreskin," she would have known that someone was trying to reach her. Doesn't that make you wonder about the important message you never got?

I bring this up not to disparage the inefficiencies of government employees, but as prelude to the most important lesson you will ever learn. It is the most fundamental and immutable law of human relations.

The sender of the message is <u>always</u> responsible for whether or not it is received.

Always.

The entire point of communication is to get the message delivered. If I write and no one reads it, I have not communicated. If I leave a message and no one picks it up, have I communicated? No. The message is just dust in the wind; a voice in the wilderness that may never be heard.

An associate of mine once flew from Austin, Texas to Chicago for a meeting with an agent. When the agent was a no-show at the airport, my associate called the woman. She was still in bed and said she had canceled the meeting by leaving him a voicemail message the night before. Who was responsible for his wasted cross-country trip?

For all the communication devices we have, we are by every measure less skilled at the art of communication than our grandfathers. We have reverted to monosyllabic grunts. *"Yo! Yo! Whassup?"* Soon, we will never be out of cellphone bars, but we will not know how to say anything. Our writing seems to be devolving into a hybrid of primitive cave scratching and Gregg shorthand.

Most of us take for granted that we are good communicators. But, without proper focus and some actual study of the skills necessary to foster effective communication, there is always the possibility for miscommunication. As a businessperson, you want to employ strategies that minimize the potential for miscommunication and enhance your ability to communicate more effectively with your target audience. Fortunately, there are principals and techniques that you can learn that will improve your communication ability. But first, let's take a look at the bigger picture.

There are two modes of communication: **verbal** and **non-verbal**.

FACTORS INFLUENCING VERBAL COMMUNICATION

Clarity – Is the message concise and to the point, and does it flow in a logical order?

Vocabulary – The very words you use create the message and nuance necessary to transmit complex and precise information.

Denotative meaning – This is the specific meaning of a word. For example, let us say that we describe Jack as being *determined*.

Connotative meaning – This is the suggested meaning. By saying that "Jack doesn't know when to quit," we have attached a negative connotation to his determination. If we say "Jack has stick-to-itiveness," we make his determination a positive quality.

Pacing – Is the delivery fast and excited or measured and calm?

Timing – If it seems like a bad time to launch into a topic, maybe it is.

Relevance – Communication can often be derailed or delayed by either straying from the topic or with the introduction of non-sequiturs and red herrings.

FACTORS INFLUENCING NON-VERBAL COMMUNICATION

1. Personal appearance
2. Intonation
3. Facial expression
4. Eye contact
5. Posture and gait
6. Gestures
7. Touch

Additional factors that impact both types of communication include:

1. Development
2. Perceptions
3. Values
4. Emotions
5. Sociocultural background
6. Knowledge
7. Roles and relationships
8. Environment
9. Space and territoriality

STEPS TO BECOMING A GREAT COMMUNICATOR

1. **Keep the objective in mind.** You are in a personal service business and good communication is your ultimate objective. Why? You need to get things done. Much of it requires the voluntary cooperation of others. You deal with facts and figures that have meaning and must be conveyed to the extent that the ramifications are clear to the other party. You have the responsibility of being certain that the people who rely on you are informed about the decisions they are making.

2. **Seek first to understand.** The better you understand what other people are feeling and wanting, the better you can fulfill your role as a trusted advisor.

3. **Think like a detective, not a judge.** Ask questions that are open-ended. Probe for the answers. Clarify.

4. **Listen more carefully and responsively.** (*See Chapter 11, Serving Real Estate Buyers*)

5. **Retain your perspective.** This will help you to be a better listener. See yourself outside of the dialogue rather than getting caught up in it.

6. **Take responsibility for your message getting through.** Sending an email or leaving a voice message is not communication. It is *attempted* communication and should be followed up on until confirmation of receipt is certain.

7. **Stay in character.** Never, ever, ever let them see you sweat. As a professional, it is unacceptable for your personal feelings to obscure the communication process. Displays of anger will not encourage what you need most from other people — open dialogue leading to cooperation.

8. **Be forthright.** Do not play games or manipulate. What works in other social settings will most often not work in

business. Beware the drama triangle; it may make for good theater, but it destroys relationships. Vow never to play the victim, the persecutor, or the rescuer.

9. **Maintain eye contact.** By focusing first on one eye, and then the other, you will find it easier to maintain eye contact without losing concentration. Try it; it really works.

10. **Build your vocabulary.** According to linguistic research, there are over 600,000 word forms. The average person knows maybe 20,000 words and uses about 1,500 in the course of a week. A powerful vocabulary could be your competitive edge.

11. **Take a writing course.** Numerous writing courses are available, from your local library to community colleges to senior centers.

12. **Enroll in Toastmasters.** This could be the best investment you will ever make in your life. Toastmasters is a support group dedicated to helping people become better speakers.

13. **Join a community theater.** The world of business has its own characters, roles, and scripts. Know your part, play it well, and you will be rewarded.

14. **Give examples.** Understanding is created by building upon a base of common knowledge. Frequent examples give those unfamiliar with the message many ways to understand it.

15. **Tell stories.** All great communicators have the ability to tell an engaging tale. Work on your stories.

Succeeding in business demands good communication skills. Fortunately, effective communication can be learned. You can be as good a communicator as you want to be.

Many people have a limited arsenal of communication tools because they place no value on them. Over the years, I have heard agents say things like, "Yeah, I told 'em, but they just don't get it," or "I left them a message; I don't know why they didn't show up."

Remember, the single most important principle of effective communication is that the sender of the message is always responsible for whether or not it is received. When I say responsible, I do not mean in some business practices sort of way, I mean in the real, practical life-and-death sort of way. If you are adrift on the ocean and a ship comes into view, do not whisper for help.

RECENT INNOVATIONS IN TECHNOLOGY AND UNINTENDED CONSEQUENCES

Why are you yelling at my voicemail?

On more than one occasion, I have checked my messages to discover that I have been the recipient of a prolonged, flaming voicemail from an angry or possibly drunken agent. Do not be that person. You are a professional and are required to behave accordingly. Today, in the world of the internet, your competitor could take an angry message from you and put it on his website for the whole world to hear.

What if someone else is listening?

Many professionals have home offices. It may be possible that family members, guests, and others could hear your message as you leave it. The purpose of voicemail is to leave a message in order to get a return call; it is not a dump box for five minutes of blather or angst.

Listen to the outgoing message to make sure you have the right person

In a seemingly bored and condescending voice, the following message was left on my voicemail by an annoyed female practitioner, "Well, that deal still stands, I know it's only a half million dollars." Loud sigh. Click.

That was it. No name, no phone number, and no way to even contact her as a courtesy to let her know that she had the wrong person. I have played that message back to a lot of people as an example of what not to do. To this day, I have no idea who she is, and I guess "that deal still stands."

Precede and end every message by slowly stating your phone number

Trust me on this one; it is hard to hear out there. Your recipient may not be able to write down a number, and they do not want to listen to the entire message again to get the number. Keep the message brief.

You've got mail

The good thing about email is that there is a record of what is said. The bad thing about email is that there is a record of what is said. Every email should be written as though it will be read by your enemy's lawyer, your employer, and your mother.

Gr8 deal 4 u boi

Texting may ultimately destroy writing as a communication vehicle. Too many things cannot be adequately abbreviated. Use it sparingly and remember: it is business.

The blog cometh. Be afraid; be very afraid.

Maybe there is some business advantage to carrying on an endless dialogue, but it appears to me to be outweighed by the potential to look stupid. If you blog, be sure to get your facts straight, check your spelling, and remember, it is indelible. It might be best to blog calm and sober.

Facebook follies

I know a lender who refers to himself on his social media as "an insurance and home loan ninja." But apparently, when he's not ninjaing loans, he's either drunk, dressing in drag, or exposing himself, as demonstrated by the photos on his Facebook page.

Social networking has its place, but it also has its perils

Already, crimes have been solved and jobs have been lost over the content on personal websites. Search engines will find you, and more people are searching professionals before committing to them. Remember, once it is on the internet, it may be impossible to remove every link. Think of it as your 21st century tattoo.

Celebs tweet a lot. Should you?

Yes, but probably sparingly. There are essentially two components to our craft: one is the legal and precise knowledge component and the other is the creation of customers. As a mechanism for conveying the former, the 140-character limit seems too limiting. As a tool in the customer creation process, it could be a double-edged sword. Think before you tweet.

Communication is at the heart of a professional's stock and trade. Yet too many professionals take for granted that they are good communicators and spend little or no time working on the fundamentals of communication. Commit some time every day to improving your communication skills and both business and personal relationships will be richer and more satisfying.

CHAPTER 7

THE PRINCIPLES OF NEGOTIATION

"For me, relationship is very important. I can lose money, but I cannot lose a relationship. The test is, at the end of a conversation or negotiation, both must smile."
—SUNIL MITTAL

A survey of buyers and sellers of real estate revealed that, from their point of view, one of the most valuable services real estate practitioners provide is our ability to negotiate on their behalf. From my experience, it appears that in many cases the clients are getting less than they are paying for. Are you a good negotiator? Do you frequently succeed in closing the gap between the parties' expectations and reality? Have you mastered the skills necessary to arrive at a solid meeting of the minds? Do you love the pressure and high drama of the negotiating table? Really?

More than one observer has suggested that other cultures are more comfortable bargaining and actually enjoy the social interaction as a separate benefit of the negotiation process. One possible explanation is that we are a comparatively new culture, established after the development of monetary systems.

To a certain extent, we have a "price tag" mentality. We are somewhat conditioned not to ask for concessions by that elitist quote, "If you have to ask how much a thing costs, you can't afford it."

In the absence of such "price tag" systems, the value of a thing is far from standardized. Value is the product of the deal made between the parties. This is the case in many Asian cultures where getting to know the other party is a vital part of consummating a business transaction.

For two years, I was the sales manager of a high-rise, live-work condominium in the heart of Los Angeles' Koreatown. While these observations are generalities of a culture more focused on the negotiation process, they did influence the negotiation process.

1. They mix business and pleasure. They want to get to know you.
2. They like to have several meetings.
3. Negotiating is an ongoing and multiple step process. They stall.
4. Contracts are just a starting point and mean almost nothing to them.
5. They like to try to make you impatient.
6. Even if they act angry, they will be offended if you respond with anger.
7. They ask personal questions that tend to make one uncomfortable.
8. They are extremely cautious.

These observations may manifest themselves to a certain extent in all negotiations. Now that we appear to be returning to a balanced market, they are worth considering.

NEGOTIATION SKILLS

For several years, market conditions eliminated the need to negotiate in real estate. No price was too high. Sellers had all the power. Negotiating skills had been gathering dust. Then came the declining market when the balance shifted from seller to buyer, and buyers wanted bargains and the seller would have to take whatever he could get. This added a sort of "take it or leave it" attitude to the dynamic.

THE PRINCIPLES OF NEGOTIATION

Now, in many markets there is limited inventory and the seller's market has returned. Negotiation skills are vital over the course of shifting market dynamics. Here are some thoughts to consider.

- **Empathy**
  The better we understand the other party, the more likely we are to bridge the gap between us.

- **Face-to-Face**
  The point of negotiation is to get signatures on paper. You cannot do that on the phone. You lose the benefit of eye contact and the nuances of communication, not to mention, you could have a bad connection.

- **Timing**
  Make sure you have ample time. Do not begin to negotiate until the other party is ready. No checkbook, no deal. If they leave the negotiating table without making a commitment, you will have to start all over again.

- **Self-awareness and emotional control**
  It is not personal … it is business. Do not become caught up in the emotion. Like a mediator, your goal is to get the parties to come to mutual agreement. That takes a lot of patience. It is a chess match, not a therapy session.

- **Know your bottom line.**
  What do you want? State it clearly. Work toward what is best for all parties, not just getting your way at all costs.

- **Counter everything**
  In many cases, the psychology of negotiating is not about money or a low price, it is about the security of not having overpaid or paid more than necessary. When we accept an offer, we can leave doubt. By countering even the most insignificant detail, we make

them say "yes" to us, and they are less likely to want to renegotiate during escrow or just before closing.

- **Commitment to succeed**
  Negotiating successfully requires a sort of mutual surrender. Both parties must willingly accept that, in order to find a middle ground, something must be given up. It is not really a win/win; it is a lose/lose with the greater goal of the mutual benefits of striking a deal.

- **Willingness to walk away**
  Occasionally, no middle ground can be found, and the parties cannot be brought together. Sometimes, the best deal is no deal. If you begin the process with that in mind, you will negotiate from a position of strength.

Remember to remain flexible, and look for a wide range of options. Our clients are counting on us, and negotiating is something a computer cannot do. Let's give them their money's worth.

CHAPTER 8

EFFECTIVELY MARKETING YOUR BRAND

"When everybody is somebody, no one is anybody."
—GILBERT & SULLIVAN

As we have discussed frequently, the fundamental business problem faced by all real estate practitioners is the over-abundance of look-alike, sound-alike, act-alike salespeople competing for a small number of closings. But, being a better salesperson is not the road to distinction, it is the road to anonymity.

Despite all of the sales training offered to real estate practitioners, real estate cannot be sold to anyone who is not qualified to buy it. By qualified, I mean someone who has a need, the means, the capacity, and the disposition for buying.

The need is driven by predictable life events that you have no control over. It builds slowly, taking between six months and five years to conclude. A major life event is occurring, the buyer has good credit and steady income, they have the intellectual ability, and they are realistic about what their money will buy. But, by the time that occurs, they already have done research on their own. You need to know them before they are ready.

More importantly, sellers aren't buying anything but you, and you should be putting your resources into building a referral-based business, not out trying to sell someone who is not qualified.

Remember that the key objective of your business is to create an ever-increasing number of referrals predisposed to list with you. At this very moment, someone you know is having a conversation with someone about an event in their life that will have implications for buying or selling real estate. You are not there, but if you had been marketing effectively you might be getting a call that starts out like this, "You don't know me but I was talking to…"

THE DIFFERENCE BETWEEN SALES AND MARKETING AND WHY IT MATTERS

"The aim of marketing is to know and understand the customer so well the product or service fits him and sells itself."
—PETER DRUCKER

At some point after mid-century, the real estate business began to evolve from a small community of professional brokers into large international sales organizations. Laws in most states were changed to allow an apprentice or salesperson to operate under the broker's close supervision. The business shifted away from providing professional real estate services and into a competition for salespeople. A broker could only do so much, but an army of salespeople splitting 50-50 with the broker became a better business model. If bigger is better, why not go for worldwide dominance?

The crowning event in this evolution occurred in 1995, when Hospitality Franchise Systems bought Century 21 to add to its stable of marketing and motel franchising companies. Despite the low margins, the executives loved the cash flow, felt they could further develop the value of the brand, and had investors' money to burn. They set out to buy every real estate agent in America. Soon they also purchased Coldwell Banker and ERA. They were buying brands knowing that agents were likely to stay, and they were right because most agents fail to develop their own identity but instead rely on the company name to give them the credibility to "close the deal."

While you may hear the terms *sales* and *marketing* frequently used together, particularly in the new home industry, they are not the same.

Selling is searching for a customer and persuading them to buy from you.

Marketing is creating a customer who comes to you, predisposed to use your services.

Marketing is two things really: it is creating the customer through identification and selection, and influencing their predisposition.

In our context, marketing can be defined as <u>taking and holding a piece of a person's mind such that any time they think of real estate, they recall your image</u>.

Remember, marketing is mental positioning. As stated earlier, take and hold the No. 1 position in the minds of 200 people (your "community") such that anytime they think of real estate or real estate finance, your image comes to mind immediately. If you cannot immediately get the No. 1 position, take the No. 2 position and be consistent. Eventually, that No. 1 position will become open and you will fill it quite nicely.

Marketing and advertising are not synonymous

Advertising may well be part of the marketing strategy, but traditional advertising can be expensive because of its broad reach.

If you have 2,000 sweaters for sale, you might run an ad in a local newspaper. But, if you have unlimited quantities of bland beer to sell, you might well spend a fortune trying to convince a certain percentage of the population that your beer is better by advertising during televised sporting events. That is *mass* marketing; you probably cannot afford it, so why bother? You have a limited supply of **you** to offer, which is further limited by geography. Advertising is not always effective or necessary, particularly in building a referral-based personal services industry.

Your marketing is a one-on-one building process; creating customers through consumer education allows you **to compete in the mind of your community, rather than in the more costly and difficult general marketplace where clutter abounds.** Still, you want to distinguish yourself. You want to build a reputation within your community for being terrific. Getting attention is a vital part of effective marketing. You must stand out from the herd.

BRANDING

In the early days of our westward migration, there were no barbed-wire fences or cattle gates. There were endless, unfettered hectares of scrub and grassland as far as the eye could see, and nothing to inhibit movement or maintain control. With so much free forage and a hungry, growing nation to feed, cattle ranching soon replaced hunting the all but extinct bison.

Unlike bison, cattle have owners. But, when you get a lot of something in one place, be it cattle or real estate practitioners, they have a tendency to be indistinguishable from one another. With no fences to keep your cattle in and another vaquero's cattle out, they would get all mixed up together and it could be very difficult to identify and cull out your steers when the time came.

I have pointed out that in many real estate markets the number of agents exceeds the number of closings by as many as five to one. When you do the math, you realize that at any given time, 80 percent of all licensees cannot possibly earn a living. What separates those who survive and ultimately succeed in building a viable, profitable, predictable business is an understanding of business fundamentals such as planning, budgeting, and time management. But in the end, their most formidable business challenge will be to distinguish themselves in an impossibly crowded field.

Crest did not have salespeople in the toothpaste aisle at the supermarket, but their marketing produced enough people who went down that aisle predisposed to look for the Crest brand to make it the No. 1 selling dentifrice in the country for 30 years. Here is an important lesson about the strength of brands: although it was the dominant brand in its product category, today it is No. 2, behind Colgate. In trying to capitalize on the strength of the brand, the makers of Crest rushed a host of other products to market.

As it turns out, market share is inversely proportional to the number of products under the brand umbrella. Automakers are learning that lesson now. Marketing cannot create more customers for toothpaste without creating more teeth.

Budweiser is not really the best beer in America, but it is a fantastic marketing company that knows the most mundane details of their young male target, how, where, and when to reach him, what images to use to plant the message, and what trigger devices to use to affect the predisposition to acquire Budweiser.

Although Century 21 is the first business most people think of when they think real estate, it isn't even in the real estate business. Like other now REALOGY companies and national firms, they are in the more lucrative agent recruiting business. The once close supervision of a broker has been replaced by that of office sales managers or franchise operators.

The reinforcement of real estate brands has made them very effective marketers to sales agents, but not particularly efficient when it comes to attracting customers, training their agents or delivering real estate services through their sales people. Effective marketing of *their brands* serves to attract a steady stream of new real estate licensees who incorrectly perceive that the strength of the *company brand* will compensate for their lack of credibility, knowledge, experience, and customers. In a sort of cruel irony, prior to departing the business, the licensee will probably spend more time and energy marketing the *company brand* to strangers than marketing *his brand* to his community.

Just as revealing is the fact that, although the company is successful because of its brand marketing, it trains its licensees to be salespeople, not brand developers. That would of course conflict with and dilute the *company brand,* and if the licensee succeeds, he will probably go out on his own and take his teeth with him. Remember, they are not in the real estate business, that is still local; they are in the agent aggregation business.

Marketing takes time. Selling is easier to teach than proficiency in the real estate business. But, in the end, marketing allows you to spend more time with the customers and referral sources of your choosing. You developed them, and no one else can advertise them away from *your brand.* Marketing your brand to your community rather than being dependent on the warm leads of your company is in line with how the role of brands has changed.

According to John Hagel, chief strategy officer at entrepreneurial operating company 12 Entrepreneuring Inc. in San Francisco and the author of *Net Worth: Shaping Markets When Customers Make the Rules,* "We are on the cusp of a major shift in how we think about branding. Historically, a brand has been a promise that says, 'If you buy this product or buy from my company, you can rely on me because of the attributes attached to the brand'. We're going to see a new kind of branding emerge, a much more customer-centric branding where the promise is, 'I know you as an individual customer better than anyone else, and you can trust me to assemble the right products or services to meet your individual needs'."

Consider for a moment the possibility that the best brand for you might be your name and image. Are you known within the community where your referrals will come from?

Defining the result

As a real estate practitioner, good times or bad, you want a nice fat portfolio of well-priced listings because some of them will sell every month. Doesn't it make sense to market in a way that produces that result?

FIRST-TIME SELLER

That is why I coined the phrase, "First-time seller." Entry-level housing always sells. Owners don't like where they live; they are just waiting for someone to show them how to move up into a better community, school district, or bigger house. If they bought the house two, three, or four years ago, they probably do not remember much so they are very easy to work with. Establish in the minds of your community that you are the trusted advisor in all matters related to real estate.

IDENTIFYING THE TARGET MARKET

You cannot be all things to all people, but you can be very special to a few if you choose wisely. Chances are that you already know a few hundred people, but part of the daily grind of real estate is adding new people to your community who are likely to refer your preferred client to you.

You only need one or two hundred people who believe in you and have your brand registered in their brain to maintain that listing portfolio. Think of it as a process of selecting and upgrading. These people are the gateway to the actual sellers. Make sure your brand will resonate with these people.

INCORPORATING YOUR UNIQUENESS AND STRENGTHS INTO THE BRAND

You are a one of a kind; there is nobody else like you. Walt Disney once remarked that what makes us unique is what makes us valuable. Your brand should reflect your uniqueness and strengths. These are the qualities that will help differentiate you and attract to you people of similar values and interests, who in-turn will refer to you people like them.

Seize a niche

Do you love golf? Why not learn every golf course and associated housing opportunity within an hour's drive? Speak about it, write about it, and of course, build your brand around it.

Consider a slogo

A slogo combines a slogan, a logo, and a graphic such as a photo into one easily identifiable symbol.

Avoid logo conflict

Maybe it only seems like everybody is branding everything, but when it comes to clothing, many people are starting to resemble a NASCAR entry. If you have more than one logo in the same vision field, it will probably be counterproductive. Personally, as my own form of personal protest, I refuse to wear anything with someone else's name on it.

Clever, not corny

There is a very fine line here. You want your brand to be memorable, but to also stand the test of time. What seems cute and clever today might seem odd in a few years. Do not be disinclined to seek the help of a professional in what might be the most important decision you ever make about your business. In the end, you, not the brand, still have to be that trusted advisor, who, in the words of John Hagel, author and former consultant, is trusted to provide the best products and services.

Junk is not marketing

A fortune is spent every year in the name of marketing on notepads, key chains, calendars, newspaper ads, etc. In my experience it is mostly an unnecessary expenditure, ineffective, and often simply a concession to ego.

There is nothing more fun than sitting at the table with a couple of homeowners, completing the listing paperwork while you both jot down notes on your competitor's notepads as her picture smiles back at you. If everybody is doing it, it is probably not the best way to differentiate yourself. It comes across as timid, passive, and unimaginative.

There are no shortcuts. Every referral is earned through a combination of regular and repetitive positive human interactions and consistent follow-up. It is your job to cultivate an extremely positive reputation within your community.

CONSUMER EDUCATION IMPARTS REAL VALUE

In my experience, consumer education is the most effective form of marketing with the purpose of obtaining listing referrals. Among the activities that I have pursued are publishing articles about real estate, monthly in-office workshops focusing on market conditions and other real estate related topics, radio programs, using an RV mobile-office, and numerous public appearances.

One of the reasons this approach is effective is that very few practitioners know enough to put themselves out there as authorities. They can talk it, but they cannot walk it.

There is no down side to learning as much as you can as quickly as you can and being able to present information in a thorough and entertaining manner. You will build confidence and learn to exude it.

PRESENTATIONS AND DIALOGUES

Most new agents do not know what to say or even what information to present. Everything said in the course of your business should be thought out well in advance. I have heard all of the excuses to resist learning a script, and none of them are valid in the slightest.

"Oh, I want to be more natural," or "Oh, I just wouldn't feel comfortable giving a canned presentation."

Face-to-face meetings are hard to get and afford no time to practice. Winging it will lead to disaster and a missed opportunity.

At minimum you will present information regarding market conditions, the buying and selling process, what to expect, and the components of the closing process. (*See Chapter 9 for information on listings and market conditions for those presentations*). You will want to have an ironclad referral presentation. Of all of the marketing you do, nothing is more important than the delivery of a referral presentation.

EFFECTIVELY MARKETING YOUR BRAND

The point of meeting people is not to "do a deal today," but to illicit their voluntary support in reaching your goal. They must know that you have a goal and understand how they can help you achieve it. Think of the thousands of top amateur athletes who get the glory while relying on a host of volunteers to make their victories possible. Goals inspire and attract.

The referral dialogue must be face-to-face to be fully effective. Breakfast and lunch are both good times. The dialogue has several elements and, to be effective, should be closely adhered to. Here is the opening phrase: "I have a goal of building a 100 percent referral-based business, and I know that with your help, I can do it. According to statistics, seven out of every 100 homeowners sell their houses annually. I'm sure you know at least a hundred people and I was wondering if you would have any objection to referring those seven people to me?"

Wait for their response. Hopefully, if they have any objection, they will use the opportunity to tell you. They could have a friend or relative in the business or they may have doubts about you. But remember, even if they say they will, does not mean they will follow through. View this as the first step in developing a referral source even if you are momentarily relegated to the No. 2 position

The next part of the referral dialogue is intended to address their unspoken concern.

"Look, I know that you are taking a risk anytime you refer someone, but I want you to know that anyone you recommend me to will receive the utmost in courtesy, quality and integrity, and I will never forget where that business came from."

That is a commitment to deliver.

The final step of the dialogue is intended to pave the way for follow-up.

"I appreciate your commitment to my goal of building a 100 percent referral business, would you have any objection if I contacted you from time to time to check up on those referrals?"

Send a note, email, or text within three days to thank them and remind them. Make a follow-up call within three weeks. They are busy; they will not think of you so you need to stay in touch. Continue to send real estate information. If they are also homeowners, send a regular CMA suggesting that they use it to make sure they have adequate insurance and to remind them that they have equity that they might wish to further invest when the time is right. That's marketing.

CHAPTER 9

BUILDING LISTING INVENTORY

"Old real estate brokers never die, they just grow listless."
—AN OLD REAL ESTATE BROKER

The real estate industry does not make much of a distinction between buyers and sellers of real estate as though they were somehow two sides of the same coin, which they are not. A listing is a legally binding contract that will almost always lead to a payday in the not too distant future. But even more importantly, a listing can be exploited to produce more listings and referrals while helping you gain market dominance in a geographic community. A listing allows you to do something that a merchant could only dream of; you can now legally place your name and image right out on the street and you can put dozens of signs up on the weekend.

Like the merchant, the single most important goal of your real estate business is to build an **inventory** of salable listings. If you have listings, you have a contractual relationship to receive compensation. Serving buyers is not as certain as representing sellers.

FIVE REASONS YOUR ENTIRE FOCUS SHOULD BE ON OBTAINING LISTINGS

1. There is an extremely limited supply of real estate and a correspondingly high demand. There are lots of unqualified buyers willing to spend all of your time hoping you can find them a miracle. Everyone wants to own real estate so by listing property, you will have your pick of the most qualified buyers.

2. Listings are your security. Build and maintain an inventory of five to 10 listings, and you will never worry about money again.
3. Listings create marketing opportunities.
4. Listings attract other listings.
5. Listings sell whether you are working or on vacation.

Buyers will be part of your business, but you must be much more selective about whom you accept. In most communities, buyer/broker agreements are still not widely used. Part of the reason is that it represents an almost insurmountable obstacle to an inexperienced agent who cannot offer a single compelling reason why that potential buyer should commit to using them exclusively.

As part of my work, I search a lot of agent websites to see how they are representing their brand. In most cases, when I click on the ubiquitous "My Listings" tab they either have none or have listed someone else's.

Sure the MLS is full of listings, but finding homes for buyers is not really your job. **Your job is to take and hold a place in the consciousness of several hundred people such that anytime they think about real estate, your image comes to mind ... and listing referrals follow.**

If you cannot do that, you cannot earn a living in real estate for any prolonged period.

Five marketable listings

Never forget that the key to a rewarding real estate career is to always maintain a minimum of five active, marketable listings. By marketable, I am referring not only to curb appeal, price, and spit and polish throughout, but also to the property's ability to contribute further listings to your portfolio. You will from time to time obtain listings that do not meet all of the criteria to be considered marketable. Although some of them may close, they are not your true objective.

The importance of proper pricing

Never, ever, no matter what, represent a property that is not priced perfectly to the market. It is malpractice of the worst order. The most likely buyers will never even know the listing exists. Buyers are generally qualified according to a price range, and agents show only those properties within that price range that meet the buyer's needs. The last thing the agent wants is to have the buyer fall in love with a house they cannot afford, so they won't even show it. Buyers who do see it will immediately realize that, in their price range, far better properties are available. It will become the comparison by which other, better houses will be valued and sold.

THE CRITICAL ROLE OF THE CMA

The result of an overpriced listing is that the real buyers never get to see it at all. You will do harm to your reputation when the property does not sell, and someone else's sign will go up.

The only thing the seller really needs from a listing agent is the perfect price. That price is the price at which the home will sell almost immediately and obtain for the seller the maximum net equity proceeds. I call that the "sweet spot." In that regard, sellers' price expectations are irrelevant. A thorough analysis of market conditions speaks for itself. A **Comparative Market Analysis (CMA)** is a science you must master; it is a combination of facts, experience, and strong intuition presented in a way that edifies and entertains.

The only person over whom you will have any influence is the seller. You won't ever get to explain to the buyer, who is represented by another agent, why the home is worth more than comparable others. The seller's ultimate willingness to "come down later" or "negotiate" will not solve the problem of the right buyer being precluded from seeing an overpriced listing. The house sells when the listing is taken, not when a dumb enough buyer comes along. But, even in the case where a buyer stumbles upon the home and agrees to pay the higher price, it would have to be an all cash transaction, since the financing appraisal will kill the loan.

A Comparative Market Analysis is the single most important part of the listing process, and your scheduled weekly activities should include presenting a bare minimum of three each week. If you want to get a listing, you must present a CMA. Before any listing agreement is signed, it is preceded by a presentation of the CMA. Do not aim at listings; you cannot hit them from here. Aim to present as many CMAs as you can and get fabulous at it. Practice, record yourself, and practice some more.

How do you get a marketable listing? Present a CMA. To see how listings develop, let's look back at how we got here.

- Before the listing was the CMA.
- Before the CMA was the scheduling of the appointment to present the CMA.
- Before the scheduling of the CMA presentation was the receiving of the referral.
- Before the receiving of the referral was the asking of the question, "Who do you know who might be thinking about selling their home?"
- Before the asking of the question was the marketing that created your image in someone's mind.
- And before any of that a significant and usually predictable event occurred in the life of someone who is known to someone you know.

Seven out of 100 homes sell each year. Roughly extrapolated, if you know 100 homeowners and you obtained a marketable listing from each one who sold annually, that would only be seven listings; in most markets you would need to double that to earn a living.

Is your goal to double the number of people you know? Yes! But, even that assumes you will get every listing, which, of course, you will not. If you see all 100 people as a source of business, you will be disappointed and probably fail. If instead, you view your 100 people as gatekeepers to the 100 people they each know, your path is clear.

Over time, the regular maintenance and improvement of your community will become the foundation of a business that can and should improve, year after year. At the same time, you want to target a specific community of homes and become an expert dominating the area. Do not leave this to chance. If you go about this properly, the first listing will lead to others in the same community, so choose wisely. This is your bread and butter, and you will spend a lot of time here.

Select a community of 300-500 homes. It could be a sprawling subdivision with multiple types of homes, a towering high-rise, a square block of stacked flats, or several blocks of bungalows on grid streets.

Factors to consider when selecting your community

1. Desirability of the community
2. Annual turnover
3. Equity
4. Where your friends and acquaintances live

I tend to target new construction because then you start out with zero competition. Most onsite sales agents are prohibited from relisting and competing with the builder's inventory; and yet, recent buyers who are forced to sell usually approach the onsite agents first.

Although most sales agents reckon that it will be a longtime before any of these new buyers resell their homes, they are often wrong. The same major life events that impact the lives of everyone are impacting them; some have no choice but to sell. In my experience, some people buy a new home to mask a shortcoming in their relationship. But ultimately, the focus on the new home dims a little and the relationship problems can often become magnified.

This serves to remind us that no matter how hard you work, your activities have little to do with the number of listings in the marketplace. They occur for reasons beyond your control, such as the birth of a child, a job transfer, promotion, retirement, and reversal of fortune.

THREE THINGS YOU CAN CONTROL

Focus on listings

When you do work with buyers, see them as a source of listing referrals. Never forget that at any given moment, someone you know is probably speaking to someone who is thinking about selling real estate. The number of listing referrals you receive per month measures the effectiveness of your business. A minimum of 10 is a good goal.

Say the phrase that pays

"Who do you know that might be thinking about selling their house?"

It all comes down to that. In the real estate business, you will be rewarded for the frequency with which you ask that exact question in exactly that way.

Do not ask about buyers. Also, be sure not to ask, "Do you know anyone who might be thinking of selling?" The answer is almost always "no." Leave the question open-ended and they will tell you about anyone with a real estate need.

Gear all marketing to the pursuit of listing referrals

For example:

Dear Friend,

Demand for real estate remains strong in our area. At the moment, I have several anxious buyers willing to pay record prices, but unfortunately, there is not much to choose from. Who do you know that might be thinking about selling their house? I will make a $250 donation to the charity of your choice for any referral that results in business.

SETTING AND PREPARING FOR THE APPOINTMENT

The time has come. You have a listing referral from a friend.

1. Be certain all owners can be present.
2. Ask them to have all loan information and other paperwork associated with the property and keys ready.
3. Send out a pre-listing package.
4. Think like a detective; question everything.
5. Order a Property Profile from the Title Company.
6. Log on to MLS and bring up the tax record. Print the full report.
7. Run a preliminary Comparative Market Analysis.
8. Select map coordinates and print the page for presentation. Highlight those map sections in which comparable properties were considered.
9. Drive the area. Take photos of the subject property.

10. See all active listings, and drive by pending and closed sales.
11. Evaluate (See below).
12. Complete the CMA and arrive at a narrow price range.
13. Prepare the Seller's Estimate of Net Proceeds.

Setting the perfect price

Outside of building a listing inventory derived from referrals, nothing you do will ever be more important than getting the price right. The market works at lightning speed, and if the property is correctly priced it should sell within days, if not hours.

Pricing is science and art. The numbers speak for themselves, but they cannot interpret themselves. Here are some things to consider.

Window of opportunity

This listing will fit between other properties in the general price range. Is there a place where it will represent greater value than its apparent competitors?

Supply and demand cycle

Because of our monetary system there is rarely a balanced market. Swings from boom to bust tend to create greater swings in value than their replacement cost would suggest. The terms buyer's and seller's market derive from this phenomenon, and that is an obvious factor to take into account when determining current market value.

Principle of substitution

Sellers must see the market from the buyer's point of view. As long as there is a property on the market that represents

BUILDING LISTING INVENTORY

better value than the seller's, that one must sell before theirs. If something better comes to market after the property is listed, the seller will either need to adjust or accept a longer market period.

Cost per square foot

Generally speaking, within a defined area, there is usually an average cost per square foot being paid for similar properties

Percentage of selling price to listing price

If buyers are paying 93 percent of the asking price, it tells me one thing. If it is 99 percent, that tells me something else. A market in which sellers name their price is a rising market and the key to a quick sale is to mark it to the market either way. Many times I've come in high because I could see that there was no better choice on the market at that price and prices had been rising. Naturally the sellers were elated, but had I been wrong it would have cost them dearly.

Unique features

Evaluating large tracts of similar homes may require less work because there are fewer variables. Some properties have unique features that need to be considered in determining the market price. Does a pool always add value? Is the granny flat permitted? Unique features sometimes come with problems that negate any increase in value. Buying a house with a pool in drought-struck areas does not seem like a very good idea.

Organize the presentation

- Tax printout – Ask them if the information is correct.
- Map page – Show them where they are on the map and how the surrounding area impacts property values.

- CMA – This reflects a snapshot in time of current market activity. It shows what other choices a buyer has, what buyers are currently paying, and what they are unwilling to pay. The objective of pricing is to get the highest possible price in the fewest number of days.

Listing information is available to anyone at warp speed. The longer it remains on the market, the more dependent it becomes on the market to change. Either the most attractive alternatives must sell or deficient properties must come to market at a higher price.

Being intimately familiar with the competition will allow you to judge from the buyer's perspective which alternatives offer the most for the money. Being the greater value is finding the sweet spot, the right balance between sales price and desirable features.

Additional documents you'll need

- Agency Disclosure
- Transfer Disclosure Statement
- Exclusive Authorization and Right To Sell
- Electronic Key Safe for demonstration of security features
- Listing Back-up Book

IT'S SHOWTIME!

Your presentation is your showcase. Arrive 10 minutes early and collect your thoughts. Make sure you are at the door on time.

1. Tour the house, make notes, and ask questions.

2. Find a comfortable place to sit (the kitchen table is good).

BUILDING LISTING INVENTORY

3. Assume the role of consultant – **Determine the true motivation for selling (if you do not already know).** Immediately take the position that you will do everything you can think of to prevent them from having to sell an appreciating/declining asset at this time. This takes you out of the role of salesperson and moves you to the position of trusted advisor. Holding property for even six more months could mean thousands of dollars to them. If selling is the appropriate course of action, move to the pricing phase.

4. Present Agency Disclosure and obtain signatures.

5. Present the CMA – Explain the tax and map pages and where the information came from. Give it validity; your entire success depends on the sellers understanding your theory of value.

6. Present the net sheet – Disclose all costs and explain each. Use your Listing Back-up book. In almost every case, the single most important question in the mind of a seller is, "How much money am I going to get?" They have done a little bit of figuring in their head and their expectations are almost certainly overly optimistic. The purpose of the entire presentation is to close the gap between those expectations and reality. Present the listing agreement and obtain signatures.

7. Demonstrate key safe.

8. Discuss staging and showing. Talk about any repairs that are needed.

9. Suggest a property inspection – Disclosures were unheard of when I entered the real estate business, and I feel fortunate to have been part of a slow and ongoing process rather than coming into that mountain of

documents as a new agent. California has a required Transfer Disclosure Statement that must be completed by the seller and provided to the buyer. From this document evolved the property inspection industry. A "qualified" individual does a thorough physical inspection of accessible areas and reports upon the conditions he finds.

Part of the evolution of the industry is the implementation of new requirements. The questions of a property inspection report are when should it be done and who should pay for it. The custom locally is that the buyer pays for it if he or she wants it. The argument is that if the seller pays for it, it could be considered to be an inducement.

I disagree. Isn't a degree of certainty about the condition of the property an important consideration in establishing market value? I believe an inspection should be done as part of the listing process and that it tends to show good faith. From a transaction management view, negative issues in a property report can scare off potential buyers when, had they been addressed or at least disclosed prior to the buyer making an offer, they may not have been a problem.

10. Complete the Transfer Disclosure Statement.

11. Explain communication – I'm not an EMT, and I am not on call 24/7. But, being on call 24/7 is only necessary if you are not any good at what you do. Despite the fact that everyone seems to be on their phone all the time, people still complain that they cannot get ahold of their agent.

    I lower everyone's expectations by promising to return all of my calls within 24 hours. That gives me time to evaluate the situation before I get back to them. I do not take many calls because I am almost always busy. People really do understand that.

BUILDING LISTING INVENTORY

Listings are the business. Buyers require a substantially higher commitment of time. A buyer will require five to 10 times the amount of time that a listing will. The time with a buyer is spent mostly showing homes that they are not going to buy. Representing buyers limits your income.

A listing that is priced correctly will sell quickly. It will take approximately three hours of research and preparation for the presentation, two hours to present the information and execute the contract, another two hours to present the offer and execute the contract, and three hours of follow-up to close.

How long will it take you to get your next listing?

CHAPTER 10

AN OPEN HOUSE WITH A PURPOSE

"No plan can prevent a stupid person from doing the wrong thing in the wrong place at the wrong time — but, a good plan should keep a concentration from forming."
—CHARLES E. WILSON

It is a familiar weekend scene in American neighborhoods, the ubiquitous open house; three signs, a flag, and one seriously bored agent watching Rachel Ray reruns in the family room.

It is apparent from the open houses I have visited that many agents do not know why they are there. Many are newer to the business (more on that in a moment) and, in all likelihood, the home they have selected is not their listing. Their behavior suggests that they believe that someone is actually going to walk through the door and buy the house. With that view of their mission, it is no wonder that they come to view open houses as a waste of time.

The true purpose of an open house is neither to sell the home nor to "pick up" a ripe buyer or placate the seller. The purpose of an open house is to build listing dominance in the neighborhood surrounding the home. You will get potential buyers just as you would if you had aimed at them. The purpose of an open house is to get multiple appointments to present CMAs.

SELECT THE RIGHT COMMUNITY

If you do business in a region where there is reasonably priced new or newer construction, you might want to consider focusing there. Depending on the age of the homes, there may have been few, if any resales, and no other agent or brand will have established dominance.

If there is ongoing advertising by the builder, so much the better in terms of traffic, but you do not need to advertise at all. Most buyers drive through areas they are interested in.

Become an expert in every floor plan, square footage, builder features, and amenities. Know the competition; know nearby communities with market values slightly lower and slightly higher than your target community. The design of newer communities also often features limited access so you can concentrate signage for maximum effect.

Choose an area that you can be enthusiastic about. Your intention is to focus your listing activity in this community, so you had better like it. The open house is how you get your toehold in the community. The open house allows you to begin to reinforce your marketing. The open house generates CMA appointments.

SELECT THE RIGHT HOME

While luck and signage will bring buyers to the home, your real goal of obtaining future listings requires that you send the right message to residents who will be sellers in the future. This is your showcase. You want it to look, feel, and smell great. Fresh paint, spruced up landscaping, clean windows, and no clutter are important evidence of what kind of advice you give sellers. Look for a home that is located near well-traveled streets.

ENSURE SUCCESS

The success of your open house should not be measured by how many possible buyers you picked up; the success of your open house should be measured according to the neighbors you have made a positive impression upon. Think of it as a low-key block party — you want the neighbors to stop in. If you want people to come to your party, you have to invite them. Run a title search and make a street-by-street list of owners. If the mailing address is different from the property address, it may be a rental. No problem, you are just looking for information. The residents of the community are people that you need to meet eventually, and a proper open house provides a wonderful opportunity.

I like using a three-pronged approach to getting neighbors to come to an open house: tell them you will be inviting them, invite them, and then remind them.

1. **The Pre-invitation**
   Sure, you could just mail them an invitation, but what if they do not come? Not only have you wasted a stamp, but you have made no progress in your quest to meet them. Walk the area between 10 a.m. and 12 p.m. on the Saturday morning the week prior to your open house and knock on doors. The following is an example of how your conversation should go:
   "Hi, I'm Ben Selling from Super Realty. Next Saturday, we are having a little barbecue across the street to help the owners sell their home. If you are interested, I could send you an invitation with all the information."
   Wait for it…it's either going to be yes or no. If yes…
   "Oh good, let me just confirm everything. "You are Mr. Skeptical. Do you prefer I contact you by email?"
   You already have their address, but you want to build

a database you can market to, and email is fast and free.

If not interested…

"No problem. Just in case you might know someone who is interested, I have prepared a price analysis; may I leave a copy with you?"

Just to get rid of you, they will take it. It is a first step in the marketing process and it allows you one more shot.

"By the way, I routinely prepare similar reports in the area for other sellers, as well as neighbors who are refinancing and people wanting to make sure their property insurance is adequate. Is that something you might be interested in?"

Wait for it.

Continue through the neighborhood to talk to as many neighbors as you can about the barbecue. You won't get them all, ever.

2. **The invitation**

It needn't be anything fancy. Include the basics: where, when, what, and why. Put the family name and property address on the invitations and hit the neighborhood on Wednesday afternoon. If no answer, either leave it at the door or come back the next day and try again.

3. **The reminder**

The morning of the event make one more round of the area to try to get those you missed and to remind those you were able to get previously.

SIGN PSYCHOLOGY

An open house is a legal excuse to plaster the neighborhood with your name. Sign restrictions in most communities would never allow you to post signs all over the area, the exception being real estate open house signs. Some communities also prohibit those and others have tried, so if you can do it, do not be stingy.

Signs, signs, everywhere signs. Signs that say who you are, signs that say how hard you work, signs that reach people at a subliminal level and make them say, "Wow, This Ben Selling really seems to be the go-to guy around here."

Put them where they will be seen by the neighborhood, not to get looky-loos to the property. Saturday is errand and kid's recreation day. People are back and forth more times on Saturday than during the week. Experiment with both Saturday and Sunday and see which day has the busiest traffic. I have seen agents holding open houses during the week, and though that may work in some communities, I doubt that they will get the same payoff as a weekend open house. With each subsequent open house, you have an opportunity to try to meet other neighbors and reinforce the impact of your signs.

AT THE OPEN HOUSE

Guest book

Unless you already know the visitors to the open house, ask them to register in your guest book as per the seller's request. Have a column for email.

Display

Create a display of relevant and interesting community information. An open house tour can sometimes turn into a sprint through the kitchen and bedrooms and a hasty exit. You got them to your open house and now you want to amuse, amaze, surprise, and delight them with information.

AN OPEN HOUSE WITH A PURPOSE

Food

You can go as fancy as you want to, but hot dogs on the grill, chips, water, soda, and coffee are all you really need. The idea is to slow them down so you can find out who they are and why they are there.

Loan officer

Have a loan officer there to talk to potential buyers about financing, and to split the setup, hosting, and cleanup chores.

Handout

Create a handout of the attributes of other available properties without the addresses. As they compare the features and benefits of other nearby properties, they will inquire about those that best meet their needs. This will help you get an idea about who they are and how they fit into your business plan.

Remember, the purpose of the open house is to attain listing dominance in an area that will benefit your business. The right property is a golden opportunity. The more you exploit that opportunity, the better. The effort you put in and the frequency and location of your signage will make its way into the minds of area residents. When they think real estate, they will think of you. *(See Appendix A)*

CHAPTER 11

SERVING REAL ESTATE BUYERS

"Buyers are liars and sellers are worse."
—A BITTER, OLD REAL ESTATE AGENT.

One of the unfortunate things I have observed over the years is the tendency to blame the consumer for an inability to create a meeting of the minds. The inability to consummate a transaction with a buyer is the result of two things: no written contract and a poor presentation.

In many communities, the use of Buyer/Broker Agreements is not yet commonplace, and a buyer's perception of the marketplace is very far from reality. They see the community as an endless sea of homes and have no concept of the limitations of the marketplace, such as total number of homes in existence or total number available for sale. They do not know that the most desirable homes may be held in families for generations and never come to market in their lifetime.

Buyers will shop agents, hoping the next one can find them the "perfect" home. Building loyalty is essential and still not entirely reliable considering that a buyer might have the best of intentions and still walk into an open house and never take your calls again.

Never lose sight of the primary objective of your business: **to build a steady stream of listing referrals.** By no means should you take all of them. For example, reject any that are not priced to market; that is a problem you cannot solve, and taking it will be a hit to your reputation.

In the pursuit of listing referrals, you will also generate potential buyers from your activities; and here again, being prepared to reject some, maybe most, is a sound business strategy if spending resources on them in any way would impede progress on your main objective.

The phone rings. You answer and a cheery voice you don't recognize says, *"We are planning to sell our condo and buy a house with a yard, is that something you might be able to help us with?"*

Your response, *"Well, why don't we get together and talk about that? What would be better for you, tomorrow afternoon or Monday morning?"*

The opportunity in a call like that is where you want to spend your time and energy. I do not want to have this conversation on the phone; I want to meet them face-to-face so I can make a presentation that will drive our relationship going forward.

THE INITIAL CONSULTATION

Every first meeting is always a consultation. This should be the real estate version of paying it forward; creating better-informed consumers. You are a consumer education advocate doing your job. It may result in signatures on a contract; it may not. But, if you can communicate interesting information in a way that benefits the person you are talking to, it will lead to good things for your business.

ASK QUESTIONS, SHUT UP, AND LISTEN

Real estate agents have a reputation for too much talk and not enough action. That is because they neither know what to say or what to do, so they talk. They talk about themselves too frequently and often too loudly. But, you are about to get information as well as give it, and the best presentation can be achieved through the "cheerleader method."

In my high school the cheerleaders were adored by everyone, from dorks to jocks. They were approachable and tended to reach out to everyone. They were always visiting hospitals and hosting fundraisers, and there was much to be learned from the fact that they went out of their way to be nice. We all should — particularly business owners focused on listing referrals.

These girls did not just get to be cheerleaders. We all grew up together, so it wasn't awe. There was something more; some intangible thing that made you see them more as individuals than members of a group doing things together.

I was curious and so I asked, *"Linda, what makes the cheerleaders so popular?"*

She paused for a moment, smiled, and said, *"Well, outside of the fact that the entire squad is drop-dead gorgeous, it's really our job to get along with everyone and make others feel good about themselves. We can talk to anyone because we just ask them questions about themselves."*

Years later I have come to understand that this was empathy. In light of the fact that real estate activity is driven by major life events, empathy, a genuine interest in the well-being of others, is an important quality to possess. Gathering information allows you to incorporate it into your presentation and tailor it to what you have learned about others.

In most markets, it is not as much about finding the "perfect" house for the buyer as it is lowering their expectations until they accept reality. That is an important distinction because you will spend all of your time hoping to find something that does not exist if you search for the perfect house, when you could be educating the buyer about the marketplace.

This was made perfectly clear to me early in my career. I was contacted by a couple from Kansas who was relocating to San Diego and needed to buy a house. I picked them up at the airport, took them to their hotel, waited while they checked-in and freshened up, and then off we went to find them the "perfect" house.

We hit it off right away. The problem was that their price range was one rung above the bottom of the San Diego market. Every third house had a brown lawn or abandoned cars dotting the landscape. At first, we kind of laughed and joked about some of the homes. I referred to the brown lawns as "water-wise" residents and noted that there were "many auto enthusiasts recycling yesterday's treasures."

But, during the fifth showing, I saw them whispering in the kitchen. To me, this was not a good sign and so I said, "Is everything OK?"

The woman said, "We like you, George, but we don't understand why you're not showing us the good ones."

Back in Kansas they had a 4,000 square foot brick home on seven acres, and I'm showing them 1,200 square foot bungalows on postage-stamp sized lots, in neighborhoods where all of the utility poles had been tagged.

They flew back to Kansas to see if they could cancel their escrow.

I had wasted more than an entire day, but I learned several valuable lessons. First, relocations into high dollar markets must be thoroughly vetted and are rarely worth the time, and looking for a quick paycheck is not the same as building a listing referral business.

Even locals often have unreasonable expectations, which is

why the buyers must receive a thorough education before any houses are ever seen. "Perfect" houses, depending on your market, begin around $600,000. The rest of us settle for what we can afford. That is why, before anyone gets into a car to buzz off and look at some houses, the buyer needs to be completely schooled in the details of the marketplace.

See Appendix B at the back of the book for an actual PowerPoint Presentation of a consumer workshop I conducted a few years ago for Prudential Real Estate. I did not bother to update it or change it to represent current conditions because it is more valuable as a snapshot in time. The numbers change continually and are backward looking. All markets are different in terms of the numbers.

All you need to do is define your marketplace and insert your own data. San Diego County is a self-contained marketplace. An island for all intents and purposes, bordered on the west by the Pacific Ocean, Mexico to the south, a sprawling uninhabitable no-man's land to the east, and camp Pendleton to the north. One MLS serves the entire county so the market is fairly easy to define and research. That may be your biggest challenge, but all of that information is available in some form or another in your market. Knowing it and presenting it will be vital to your success.

The buyer should sit with you at a computer or tap into your Cloud and watch you narrow the search down to the homes they will actually see. That way they know that you are not hiding the good ones. You may wind up with no homes that match the criteria they tell you to enter. Nothing says we need to lower our expectations like seeing the screen come up empty with a message that says, "There are no properties that match your search criteria." Now they will understand that it is not a search as much as it is a process of elimination.

PREQUALIFICATION

In order to find the right homes to show, you must know what they can afford. This can be tricky and delicate, but I learned the hard way how important this step is.

Back in the day, agents took shifts answering the office phone, mostly taking messages for other agents. *"No Lenny, Liz isn't here. You don't have to call every 15 minutes. As soon as she comes back, I promise I'll have her call you first thing, but I think it's gonna be awhile; the last time I saw her she was getting into her car with an apple fritter the size of a hubcap and a 64-ounce Coke."*

There was always that faint hope that when that phone rang, it would be someone responding to a newspaper advertisement and maybe you could "talk them in."

One hot day in 1979, a man and a woman in their 60s walked in to buy a house. He was gruff and to the point and told me exactly what he wanted, including a pool. He wanted to use his VA benefits and wouldn't "pay a penny over 90 thou."

The MLS was contained in a book and it showed five possibilities, but they were all in Escondido, a fair distance away and a place I had only been to once in my life. With a Thomas Brothers Map book in hand, I thought, "what could possibly go wrong?"

As we settled into my car, I handed him the map book and asked him to navigate. He immediately turned around and dropped it in his wife's lap. Neither brought their glasses.

It was a hot day and I had to pull over frequently to figure out where we were. One of the addresses we were never able to find.

THE AWFUL TRUTH ABOUT CAREERS IN REAL ESTATE AND WHAT TO DO ABOUT IT

I was unable to make an appointment at one of the homes because no one answered the phone and answering machines were uncommon in 1979. I assumed that the residents weren't home, but when we got to the front door, we could see that the house was wide open and we could hear music coming from the back of the house. I pounded repeatedly on the door but there was no response. Did they go away and leave a radio on and the front door open or were they engaged in something whereby they were not available to receive visitors? We did not go in.

After about five hot and sweaty hours of driving in circles, we had narrowed it down to one house, so back we went to the office to write the contract. Back then the entire closing file was about three pages; a one-page purchase agreement, closing cost estimate, and maybe something else.

I took them into the conference room and did an estimate of closing costs and approximate monthly payments, and since they did not have their glasses, I had to point and read. *"So, that's $90,000 at 9.5 percent interest which works out to be about $900 a month."*

He seemed to levitate above his chair for a couple of seconds; the chair rolled back and hit the wall as he bellowed, *"I wouldn't pay nine hundred dollars a month to live in the Taj Mahal!"*

He was gone so quickly I did not have a chance to point out that the Taj Mahal doesn't have a swimming pool. Prequalification would have prevented this, and I would have had a much better day.

If you arrange loans, you'll want to do this yourself. If you work with a lender, have her on standby so she can ask the delicate questions. When she is done speaking with them she will give you their price range and you will know what they can afford.

SHOW NEW HOMES FIRST

In many markets, resale agents and new home agents do not play well together. They seem to feel as though they are competitors when, in fact, what they do is entirely different. A new home sales agent goes to the same listing every day and conducts an open house hoping a buyer will come in and buy one of the "many fine homes currently available or under construction."

It's a one shot deal. They are not building relationships to generate future listing referrals; they have one product to sell and one opportunity to do it. People who come back are few and far between. That's selling.

Building a business is about doing everything in your power today so that listing referrals will flow tomorrow. A resale agent does what they enjoy doing with their ever-growing list of friends in order to obtain listing referrals. Yet, it rarely occurs to resale agents that new home sales agents are an abundant source of listing referrals. They can make your business. Many people must sell a home to buy one. Generally, new home agents do not represent sellers due to the perceived potential conflict of interest.

Visit all new home subdivisions in your marketplace. Some areas have abundant new home construction; others, none at all. If you have the good fortune to live in an area of significant new home construction, use it to your advantage.

It is very likely that your buyers will see these homes whether or not you show them. But, then they will not be registered and if they do wind up buying one, you will get nothing. Another reason to show new homes first is that it is way easier and gives you a great opportunity to get to know your buyers better. You will not have to set appointments, fumble with key safes and keys, or calm growling dogs all while trying to present the property and get to know them.

Tell them that even though these homes may not be right for them, part of their process of elimination is comparing new home offerings. It is an easier way to narrow down the endless list of options and get to what is most important to them.

I introduce the buyers to the new home sales representative and encourage the representative to present their product while I hang back and listen. When the onsite reps see that you bring buyers to their developments, they will send listing referrals to you. Unless you are in a market where builders do not offer fees to outside agents, should your buyer select one of the homes, your job is done.

THE STORY OF DISCOVERY HILLS

In 1992, I opened a RE/MAX brokerage on the borders of Vista, Carlsbad, and San Marcos in north San Diego County. The demographics could not have been more promising, and as I did my research, I realized that the area was on the cusp of a boom. California State University San Marcos had just started to develop what is now a campus of nearly 11,000 undergraduates. (See *The Silver Corridor* article in the Appendix.)

In Vista, the South Vista Industrial Area was attracting a lot of jobs, while a few blocks away the regional justice system was planning the construction of a brand new courthouse. Jobs were coming and people would need housing. Adjacent to the university campus were several hundred acres just beginning development of what would be the master-planned community of Discovery Hills, containing hundreds of homes of all types.

With years of new construction ahead, I knew that this area would be a hotbed of activity and I was determined to become an expert in Discovery Hills. I formed relationships with the new home sales representatives and almost immediately began to get listing referrals. When the first new home came back on the market, my sign was in front of it. Within a year, I listed and sold at least one floor plan in four different communities with the next year being even better.

SHOWINGS

Newer agents have asked me what they should take with them when showing property. I tell them that a large caliber handgun, a roll of duct tape, Clorox Handi Wipes, and a bottle of George Dickel whisky have gotten me through most field emergencies. I realize some people would be apprehensive about taking weapons and whisky along when showing property, in which case, I would suggest a career that does not involve going into the average American home where such things are as common as swing sets.

I recommend an abundance of caution when showing property. Be aware of your surroundings and literally be prepared for anything. I'm not a snob so I will list anything that is priced to market. Early in my career, I developed a sub-prime REO connection who fed me foreclosure listings in Lincoln Park located in what was known as Southeast San Diego.

Southeast San Diego is crime-ridden and impoverished, and the name is synonymous with street gangs, drug dealing, assaults, and homicide. I used to drive east on Imperial Avenue and turn south on Euclid to get to my listing on Solola Avenue. That corner is known locally as "the four corners of death." The area had become so notorious that a few years ago city officials banned the use of the geographic designation "Southeast San Diego" in favor of, well, nothing.

Problem solved. It is now just that "vibrant community down

there in the lower right hand corner of the county map." This is a great idea for other cities that have pockets of crime and poverty; stop talking about them and they just go away. At least they fought the urge to try to paper over the broken-window with a new name that sounds fabulous such as "Prosperity Heights," "Sunny View," "Banker's Hill," or disown it completely and call it "Northeast Tijuana."

Many residents and locals, however, still refer to the area as Southeast. Back in the day it was home to the Lincoln Park Piru/Syndo Mob and now the Lincoln Park Bloods; they call it Southeast and Lincoln Park is still Lincoln Park.

Lincoln Park was good to me. These were by far the lowest priced listings I ever had but they came regularly, sold quickly, and the client, San Marino Savings, needed someone they could trust to look after rehabs and get the homes closed. Would I have chosen that area? Heck, no! But because you never know where your real estate adventure will take you, it is always best to be prepared.

PHOTO ALBUM

One thing I found very useful was a small photo album that starts with pictures of my home, a mid-century, single level that has a lot of wood and windows and sits high on a hill by which people always seem to be favorably intrigued. I also included some lifestyle photos. I kept it in the center console of my car and at an appropriate time I say, "Oh, here are some pictures of where I live."

Once they had the album they would start turning the pages, which would prompt frequent comments like, "Oh, you play softball, I was wondering how I could get on a team."

"What position do you play?"

"Oh, you have a cat, a garden, a guitar…"

That way they feel that they know you a little better, and you can learn a lot about them to connect on mutual interests. If you receive sales achievement plaques, avoid the temptation to hang them in your car. I do not think consumers are impressed by sales success, and it can often work against you.

TOOLKIT

Just the other day I pulled into my local farm stand to get some berries, and there was a woman in an older Mercedes trying to get her trunk to stay closed. This was a great opportunity for me to make a new friend, as well as hit my target of meeting one new person every day. It all came down to a loose bolt. I got out my basic toolkit and in about three minutes, I made someone very happy. How cool is that?

At minimum, you'll need Philips and flat-head screwdrivers, pliers, a crescent wrench, a 100-foot tape measure, a claw hammer, bungee cords, wire, assorted nails, screws, nuts and bolts, a box cutter, rubber bands, and of course, the above mentioned duct tape.

SETTING THE ORDER

Once you have decided which properties to show, you will need to map a route. Some thought needs to go into this, at least to determine where to start and where to end. Three or four showings is a good number, but no more than six in one day.

There comes a time when the mind can no longer look and evaluate, and a sort of overload sets in. I get it after about two hours at the museum. Some research has suggested that the human brain can only manage three or four things at once, and with getting in and out of the car, people get tired.

You are only at each home for a few minutes, and after a while, it all runs together in a blur of doors, sinks, knick-knacks, and junk. That is why it is so critical to employ the process of elimination that I recommend below.

I generally start with what I consider the least likely and end with what I think they will see as the best value. You do not want to show several houses and ask them to make a choice. Instead, after each showing, eliminate either the one just seen or their favorite up to that showing. They should never wind up doing anything but choosing between two options.

Once you get back to the car ask, "If these were the only two houses available, which would you prefer?" Again, the focus is on the process of elimination rather than finding the "perfect" house.

WRITING THE OFFER

The time has come. There are no more houses to be shown and one survivor remains. The time to move forward is at hand. If you have set the stage correctly, the buyer will see the value and the offering price should be no issue. Do not ask them what they want to offer; tell them what you think it will take to create a meeting of the minds.

Where?

You have options here, and some real estate gurus recommend you do it while still at the home of their choice, before they "cool off." But, buying a home isn't an impulse buy. There will be obstacles enough to overcome on the way to closing, and the buyer will have ample opportunity to reject the home during the inspection process. If, after all is said and done, they just decide to walk, there isn't much that can be done about it. Sure, the contract is enforceable. You can get damages, maybe your brokerage fee, but it may take years and you still cannot make them buy the house if they do not want to. Good luck with the referrals on that one.

So, while I agree that you should move forward as rapidly as possible, for a host of good reasons beyond expediency, I see no advantage in trying to rush someone out of fear that they will change their mind if given time to think about it. To me that is the old sales culture, more appropriate for door-to-door brush sales than the complicated business of real estate.

It may be that the home itself is the best option for writing the offer if it is conducive and appropriate. Distractions are your enemy; you will be taking them through a mountain of paperwork and explaining numerous documents that you will be assisting them in completing. Whether on a portable device or on paper, you will want a place free of maple syrup, and restaurants can be noisy and filled with distractions.

You can probably work out something with a local restaurant if there is a quiet booth and ask them only to approach when you make persistent eye contact. The advantage to a self-serve restaurant such as a Starbucks is that there is no wait staff to interrupt you. I try to avoid restaurants since it takes time to go to the restroom, look at the menu, order, chat, eat, and go to the restroom again. If you have an office that you feel good about, go there. Not only do you have control, but you also have help if you need it.

GETTING TO THE BOTTOM LINE

You should already have a CMA and net sheet prepared. Do a CMA for any property you think the buyer might be interested in because you can use it to support the offering price. There is absolutely nothing wrong with recommending asking price if the CMA supports it, and it is far more likely to lead to a meeting of the minds.

Do not be a rescuer or a white knight; you get paid to close escrows, not find them the bargain of a lifetime. Those usually do not come on the market anyway as they are more likely to be purchased by people in real estate.

They may say something along the lines of, "Well, let's just try it and see what happens."

To which you should respond, "You know, Bob and Carol, I know the listing agent very well and she is very good at what she does. She understands as well as I do that if the property is listed above its true market value, it will not even be seen by the right buyers. I know that when Debbie listed that home she got the seller to come down as far as he is willing to go. Besides, it isn't like you have to come up with $290,000 or the $300,000 asking price today. You have 30 years and that works out to a difference of about a dollar a day."

"By trying to buy the home under market, you run the risk of losing the home to another buyer who sees the value, or alienating the seller such that even if we do succeed, he enters the transaction with an attitude of animosity when we need him to be helpful and cooperative, all for the sake of a dollar."

PRESENTING THE OFFER

I am old school and I believe I am doing the best job for all parties involved if I present the offer directly to the seller. For those of you representing the buyer, there is no downside, and to the seller's agent, what are you so worried about?

Don't you want someone there who can answer the seller's

questions related to the buyer's offer? Don't you want another creative mind there to suggest ways to bridge any gap between buyer and seller? Who would know better what the buyer might be willing or able to do?

You have every right to present your offer unless the seller says otherwise in writing.

If there is a counter-offer, you will need to revisit your buyer and discuss a response to the counter-offer. Buyers can be time consuming and unprofitable, but if they are highly qualified financially and understand and accept market realities, your odds of a closing will be vastly improved.

CHAPTER 12

PREDICTABLE OBSTACLES TO CLOSING AND HOW TO AVOID THEM

"Success depends upon previous preparation, and without such preparation, there is sure to be failure."
—CONFUCIUS

Whether you represent the buyer or the seller, you want to use your knowledge and expertise to prevent your transaction from failing to close. Numerous factors contribute to the failure of a contract between a buyer and seller of real estate. Financing, possession dates, disclosures, due diligence, inspections, pre-closing contingencies, local market conditions, appraisal reports, ability and competence of the practitioners assisting the clients, change in either party's personal circumstances, as well as property and neighborhood issues are among the more common contributors to a cancellation.

An all cash offer scheduled to close ASAP that waives all inspections is pretty likely to close. The maximum leveraged offer, contingent on financing from self-employed, itinerant hod carriers, scheduled to close in 120 days, attached to a sheaf of pre-closing contingencies, in a declining neighborhood with numerous drive-by shootings ... not so much. And, in the case of new home sales subject to construction completion times, the same property might cancel several times.

For this reason, it is hard to get a baseline on which to set expectations. However, having worked in both large real estate organizations, franchises, and on MLS committees, it seems that given a large volume of transactions over a period long

PREDICTABLE OBSTACLES TO CLOSING AND HOW TO AVOID THEM

enough to have been subject to all types of market conditions, about 25 percent of all contracts fail. Smaller firms with more seasoned agents tend to close about 90 percent of their written contracts.

That would seem to me, particularly in this market, a very worthwhile and challenging goal. Sure, one philosophy says if you throw a certain amount up onto the wall, some of it has got to stick, but I think that idea is so yesterday. No matter how much business you do, even a single cancellation takes a certain emotional toll. Better to use that psychic energy working toward more certain transactions than pushing a rock up a hill.

Many failed transactions never should have been written in the first place. But others, too many others, could have been saved by a little advanced planning. People in our business are perennial optimists. We have to be, now more than ever. But, when it comes to anything that could be torpedoed by one of Murphy's Laws, as professionals, it is our duty to assume that all may not go well and prepare accordingly.

DEALING WITH UNCERTAINTY

From my observations, it appears that our greatest obstacle in this market is uncertainty. Some people are in danger of losing their jobs and, as we are seeing, there is a sort of trickle-down effect. This is on people's minds, whether they think they will be touched by it or not.

There is uncertainty about value. Who wants to pay more for something if they could have saved substantial money by waiting a few months, or even weeks? Whether we want to admit it or not, there is uncertainty about our very system.

The mainstream media continues to bombard the public with

a steady stream of erroneous analysis, misinformation, and gore. "If it bleeds it leads," they say. We must counteract that by providing factual information. The first step in building a solid foundation for closing is the initial consultation. Again, whether buyer or seller, they need to understand the bigger picture.

ELEMENTS OF AN INITIAL CONSULTATION

Needs analysis

Beyond the client's interest in either buying or selling real estate are circumstances that are vital to the success of your closing. We need to understand his or her motivation and mood. Start with a simple and disarming question, "Why are you considering making a move at this time?" There are only a finite number of answers to that question but this, and not the real estate transaction, is the real need seeking to be met. Buying or selling real estate may not be the solution to the underlying need. If it isn't, you've got one strike against closing.

Recently, I did a CMA for an urban loft. There were several others listed within the building and a couple at distressed prices. Coming to market under those circumstances, I knew it wasn't likely to arrive at a fast sale. The *why* was to cash in. I advised my client to wait. I know many practitioners who would have taken that listing. Unless the seller is willing to price at market, there are too many other choices. Taking an overpriced listing in a crowded and declining market is hardly a recipe for success.

The bigger picture

Every generation faces challenges. The Great Depression, sandwiched between two World Wars, impacted three decades of my father's life. But, people had families and still needed a roof over their heads. To succeed in our business, we must be able, when appropriate, to assuage people's apprehensions about their future.

Despite the news of the moment, there is a predictable future. We are a growing and shifting nation. In the directions we are moving, there is inadequate developed real estate to support the job growth underlying the migration. For individuals buying property in the 10 growing regions, called "Megapolitans," the future is relatively certain.

Investors are active in the market. Not speculators, but investors. Why? Because they know demographics, and there is no competition. The best value is obtained when you are the only buyer.

Demographics

Some of the most important work in analyzing future job growth and corresponding migration patterns was done by Robert E. Lang, director of the Metropolitan Institute, and associate professor of Urban Affairs and Planning at Virginia Tech. Lang, working with data from the Census Bureau supported, in part, by the Brookings Institute, identified what will be the most dramatic socio-economic shift in our nation's history.

In the last three centuries, we have constructed more than 300 billion square feet of homes, offices, stores, and factories. Lang notes that it will take just 25 years to build the next 200 billion square feet. Get ready for the mother of all booms.

According to the Lincoln Institute of Land Policy, "Megapolitan areas extend into 35 states, contain less than one-fifth of all land in the lower 48 states, but captured more than two-thirds of total U.S. population." CNN Money calls it "The $25 trillion land grab…" and "…a treasure map of opportunity." Strong words for a media outlet with little expressed affection toward real estate as an investment.

Local market conditions

Buyers look into the marketplace and observe an endless sea of houses. Sellers see only one. Both must fully understand the breadth and depth of what is available, as well as the general nature of the local economy. This provides a great opportunity to discuss the MLS, how it works, the number of properties on the market, and the process of elimination.

Paperwork review

This is the best time to present the contract, disclosures, and forms that will comprise the closing process. Most people are not able to absorb a lot of details while under the stress of making one of the biggest decisions of their lives. Demonstrating the paperwork and explaining the role of each item will make it much easier for them to commit when the time comes. They won't feel like they need to pore over all those documents before pulling the trigger, so they won't be able to use that as an excuse to procrastinate. If you provide them with draft copies, they can have an opportunity to review them at their leisure and highlight anything they are uncertain about. Covering the paperwork is a great segue into the next item.

Closing process step-by-step

Many people become disenchanted by all of the steps and people involved in the closing process. By one estimate, there could be as many as 30 separate individuals involved; everything from the pest exterminator to the notary. Each has a job to do and a contribution to make to the closing process. We do not always control either the demeanor or performance of many of these people, and some we may not even meet. We need to prepare our clients by providing them with a breakdown of all the players, what they do, why they do it, and when things will occur.

Milestones

Every transaction has key points. Loan approval, inspections, appraisal, title review, and pest clearance are likely milestones. Make sure the client understands the importance of these events.

Prepare the client for ongoing documentation requests, a low appraisal, negative inspection reports, or slow performance by the other party.

Communication

Keep your client in the loop. With the availability of online transactions and escrow tracking, there is a great opportunity to bring the client right into the process. Prearrange communication by discussing it in the initial consultation. Don't make assumptions. Ask, "When I do need to communicate with you, what is the best method to reach you?"

By thinking forward and preparing the client for the inevitable ups and downs of a real estate transaction, you can be confident that you are closing every possible transaction.

CHAPTER 13

DISTRESSED PROPERTY, SHORT SALES, FORECLOSURES, AND REOS

"That's life!"
—FRANK SINATRA

We must never forget that behind every real estate transaction is a major life event. For most of us, life is a series of ups and downs, and for many of us, the last several years have been very challenging financially.

A lot of people I know lost good jobs and never got them back. Businesses saw revenues shrink while expenses grew and either closed voluntarily or could not hang on any longer. That's life. But, it is also the real estate business. Birth, death, divorce, illness, relocation, and change in financial circumstances are behind most real estate transactions.

It is inevitable that at some point in your career you will become involved with properties that face certain challenges. And so, the question will arise; should you spend your valuable time and energy on these challenges or simply avoid these situations altogether?

That depends. It is, after all, a business decision and deserves some consideration. These segments of the market can become lucrative niches, but they can also be fraught with title problems, can lead to nothing, or even wind up in litigation down the road.

If you are just beginning your career, you will face the incredible

DISTRESSED PROPERTY, SHORT SALES, FORECLOSURES, AND REOS

obstacle of how much you need to learn just to close a straightforward storybook transaction, which by the way, is exceedingly rare. I would recommend that you get some experience and give yourself time to learn about distressed transactions, as well as the red flags of which to be wary.

There have been at least 10 million homes foreclosed on in the U.S. Some experts fear we could see that many more in the years to come. The vast majority of the foreclosed loans were originated by "too big to fail" banks on Wall Street to be pooled and sold as mortgaged-backed securities (MBS).

The purpose of a mortgage-backed security is to provide the investor a high yield while promising absolute safety. Wall Street referenced their own risk analysis pointing out that historically, foreclosure rates were around 0.3 percent. But, those numbers were based on circumstances that were not present in MBS loans. Years ago, loan products were designed and made available to be paid back. These loans were designed to not be paid back. *(For a detailed explanation, see Chapter 16.)*

When you say subprime loan, most people think of unqualified borrowers. That is a total and intentional misdirection. Many people with excellent credit were steered into subprime loans. A subprime loan is designed to fail, deliberately targeted in a predatory manner, and represents a fraud upon both the borrower and the investor, neither of whom understand the true intent of the "bank."

Remember all of those multi-billion dollar settlements for mortgage backed securities fraud? Unfortunately, the deception did not end there. We also know that appraisals were inflated because the Wall Street analysts who created the new subprime mortgages noted that properties with negative equity had a higher incidence of default.

We know, as well, that the creators of these new types of loans bought insurance policies that would pay them multiple times the loan amount if a certain percentage of loans within a given pool went into default. These were called credit default swaps. We also know that many defaults were manufactured by servicers, where borrowers were current on all of their obligations. Servicers delayed the application of payments, created shortages in impound accounts, and used these excuses to push another loan into the default category.

Bear in mind that default and foreclosure are not the same thing, which is why many defaulted properties have yet to make their way through the foreclosure process. The terms of the agreements required that only a small percentage of loans in the pool, usually eight percent, would need to be in default and then the entire pool is declared to be in default.

TITLE PROBLEMS, MERS, AND VOID ASSIGNMENTS

It is important to understand that distressed properties are among the most likely to have title problems. Mortgage Electronic Registrations Systems (MERS) was created by Wall Street to facilitate the fraud and hide the players. MERS is the Wikipedia of title registries in that its Wall Street members just hired firms to fabricate the missing documents by forging new look-alikes. These documents, fabricated, forged, robo-signed, and falsely notarized were then recorded in counties all over the U.S. and used as phony evidence to steal homes that did not belong to them.

Aided by 25,000 former fry cooks, bartenders, and other minimum wage employees who signed off as vice presidents, they conspired to change the ownership records on millions of properties without any legal authority to do so by simply entering false information into their own proprietary

DISTRESSED PROPERTY, SHORT SALES, FORECLOSURES, AND REOS

alternative title registry system and subsequently filing forged documents with the county recorder.

This means that no one can demonstrate the legal right to foreclose in the first place, and it is wise to understand the implications of this when representing parties involved in the buying or selling of distressed properties such as short sales and foreclosures. Except for a few counties, everyone looked the other way. Valuable title records going back hundreds of years have been hopelessly corrupted. Approach foreclosures with caution.

Still, it is important that you learn this area because it will be a factor in every market for decades to come. It is the 800-pound gorilla of real estate.

SHORT SALES

A short sale is the residential equivalent of commercial real estate's haircut. It revolves around an agreement by the lender of record to allow a borrower to sell the property at market value and accept the proceeds that are projected to be less than the amount required to fully repay the obligation.

For a seller facing foreclosure, it could be a better alternative than doing nothing. For a buyer, there remains the lingering issue of a knock on the door someday. The acceptance and escrow period can last for months and may never close at all.

Whether seller or buyer, each must acknowledge the possibility that the party agreeing to a reduced payoff amount may have no legal authority to do so. Further, the default may be more valuable to the mortgaged back securities originators than the proceeds of a short sale.

REAL ESTATE OWNED (REOS)

Post foreclosure properties usually come back to market and someone has to list them. Since your goal is to build a steady stream of listing referrals, having an REO relationship can be very valuable since the owner is anxious to sell and has reasonable expectations regarding the proceeds. Marketing these properties can be more challenging and may also come with the responsibility for arranging for property repairs and security.

FORECLOSURES

The following information was made available by the Judicial Council of California and is provided for comparison only since foreclosure laws vary from state to state.

In California, lenders can foreclose on deeds of trust or mortgages using a non-judicial foreclosure process (outside of court) or a judicial foreclosure process (through the courts).

- **Non-judicial foreclosure** is the most common type of foreclosure in California. It is used when there is a power-of-sale clause in the deed of trust that secures the mortgage loan by giving the trustee the authority to sell the home to pay off the loan balance at the request of the lender if the borrower defaults (fails to make payments).

The One-Action Rule limits the lender to recovery of the property only. When a lender uses the non-judicial foreclosure process against a borrower who fails to pay on a mortgage for his or her primary residence, the lender gives up the right to collect a deficiency judgment against the borrower.

- **Judicial foreclosure** involves filing a lawsuit to get a court order to sell the home (foreclose). It is used when there is no power-of-sale clause in the mortgage or deed of trust. Generally, after the court orders the sale of the home, it will be auctioned off to the highest bidder.

Judicial foreclosures are rare in California. A judicial foreclosure allows the lender to get a deficiency judgment against the borrower. But, the homeowner has the right of redemption, which allows him or her to buy the home back from the successful bidder at the auction for one year after the sale. The process is longer and more costly than a non-judicial foreclosure.

Foreclosure process

These are the main steps in a non-judicial foreclosure, which apply to the majority of foreclosures in California.

1. The lender MUST contact the borrower and anyone else on the mortgage loan to assess your financial situation and explore your options to avoid foreclosure (called a "foreclosure avoidance assessment"). The lender:
   - Cannot start the foreclosure process until at least 30 days after contacting the borrower to make this assessment; and
   - Must advise the borrower during that first contact that the borrower has the right to request another meeting about how to avoid foreclosure. That meeting must be scheduled to take place within 14 days.
   - A borrower can authorize a lawyer, HUD-certified housing counseling agency, or other advisor to talk on the borrower's behalf with the lender about ways to avoid foreclosure. A borrower cannot be forced to accept any plan that the borrower's representative and the lender come up with during that discussion.

2. If the borrower and the lender have not worked out a plan to avoid foreclosure, the lender can record a **notice of default** in the county where the home is located at least 30 days after contacting the borrower for the foreclosure avoidance assessment. This marks the beginning of the formal and public foreclosure process. The lender sends the borrower a copy of this notice by certified mail within 10 business days of recording it. A borrower then has 90 days from the date that the notice of default is recorded to cure (fix, usually by paying what is owed) the default.

3. If the borrower does not pay what is owed, a **notice of sale** is recorded (at least 90 days after the notice of default is recorded). The notice of sale states that the trustee will sell your home at auction in 21 days.

    The notice of sale must:
    - Be sent by certified mail.
    - Be published weekly in a newspaper of general circulation in the county where the home is located for three consecutive weeks before the sale date.
    - Be posted on the property, as well as in a public place, usually at the local courthouse.
    - Have the date, time, and location of the foreclosure sale; the property address; the trustee's name, address, and phone number; and a statement that the property will be sold at a public auction.

4. At least 21 days after the date when the notice of sale is recorded, the property can be sold at a public auction. The successful bidder must pay the full amount of the bid immediately with cash or a cashier's check. The successful bidder gets a trustee's deed once the sale is complete. The lender usually bids at the auction in the amount of the balance due plus the foreclosure costs. If no one else bids, the home goes to the lender.

Stopping the foreclosure sale

The borrower has up to five days before the foreclosure sale to cure the default and stop the process. This is called reinstatement of the loan. During the 21-day period after the notice of sale is recorded, any person or institution (like a bank) with an interest in the home has the right to redeem the home up until the non-judicial foreclosure sale/auction. This means that they must pay the entire loan in full.

After the foreclosure

Whoever buys the home at the foreclosure sale/auction cannot just change the locks to the home. The new owner must serve the occupant with a three-day written notice to "quit" (move out) and, if the occupant does not move out in the three days, go through the formal eviction process in court in order to get possession of the home. That process, known as an unlawful detainer, typically takes several weeks.

In addition to lien and title issues, the property may also be in distressed physical condition. Anything unusual, even a pool, could complicate the sale of a property. Foreclosures also tend to suffer from deferred maintenance. Often this is the case with older homes that have not been through foreclosure.

I recall going to meet with the owner of a then 90-year-old farmhouse. It was everything you would imagine: quaint, charming, and — to my trained eye — flashing numerous warning signs. My business approach in these circumstances is to gather facts and render an opinion based on those facts. A home inspection may not reveal the extent of all problems, but it provides a great place to start. It will tell us if we need a more in-depth look at a problem.

A home inspection is relatively inexpensive and provides information necessary to establish market value and suggest a course for marketing the property. In the case of the farmhouse the seller refused to have the home inspection, and I declined to list it.

As full disclosure is always the ethical choice, the true professional will want to be aware of all issues before agreeing to represent the seller. It is good business as well, because there is a buyer for every property being offered at true market value.

Distressed properties are a normal part of the real estate market. Choosing to work in that arena comes with risks and challenges. A good sense of humor and reasonable expectations are absolutely required. Putting it in perspective, distressed properties result from adverse circumstances, and changing circumstances are what drive the need for real estate practitioners. They are part of the marketplace, but only part. Pursuing that part of the market is just a business decision.

CHAPTER 14

STRESS AND YOUR HEALTH

"To me, good health is more than just exercise and diet. It's really a point of view and a mental attitude you have about yourself."
—ALBERT SCHWEITZER

If I were the "most interesting man in the world," (and I'm not saying I'm not), I wouldn't want you to be thirsty; I would want you to "stay healthy, my friend."

Real estate is dynamic. When dealing with the lives of others, anything can happen. There will be high anxiety, drama, danger, and disappointment. That is the way of business and life, and this will be your arena with real consequences.

I once had a listing on a fixer-upper located on a great piece of property. The seller was a woman with three children who was broke. Just getting the property through escrow was a challenge. But, there we were on the eve of closing when she got a call from a lawyer who represented the ex-wife of my client's husband. Unknown to her, he owed back child support in excess of the proceeds of the sale.

Drama? Oh, there was plenty of that, and more to come. She was hysterical so I decided to drive her to the lawyer since we were only a freeway trip of about 45 minutes away. Once there, she was to sign away all but $1,500 to her husband's ex-wife.

Several times she said she would not close. I understood, but it would not have changed anything. As I explained this to her, a sort of resolve set in and she went silent. Then, she unbuckled her seat belt and tried to open her car door at 60 mph. I needed every bit of strength to hold onto the waistband on her jeans with my right hand while steering with my left. I was screaming at her to think of her kids when she finally flopped back in the seat while I made it to the shoulder of the road.

It was not a long time — 20 seconds, maybe. Twenty seconds of stark-raving terror. My heart pounds even now when I think about it. I could have lost my grip on her and she would have been killed or I could have lost control of the car in which case we would both have been killed.

Then, there was the time I locked two clients and myself inside a six-foot high, walled patio. I used the patio table to get on top of the wall and dropped down to the other side so I could go back into the house and free them from captivity. Today, we all carry cellphones, but back then, somebody had to go over the wall.

On another occasion, my assistant went to do a final walk-through on a listing of mine in San Marcos. The seller had done a nice job fixing up the home before moving away so we knew the inspection would go well. When the parties walked into the kitchen they discovered a hole had burned through the roof. A few days before, one of our infamous wildfires roared through San Marcos on its way to La Costa.

Apparently, an ember had landed on the wood-shake roof and the home began to burn. It was spotted almost immediately, the fire department was called and the fire put out. We had no idea since there was no other damage in this area, and it could not be seen from the street. There was nothing physically challenging about this, but it did produce stress. Escrows can never close soon enough to suit me. In the interim, I worry and wonder. *(See Chapter 12.)*

A buyer client in escrow on a high-end property was the chief

STRESS AND YOUR HEALTH

manufacturing executive for a cheese company. A batch of cheese was improperly made and a resulting listeria outbreak claimed several lives. He went to prison and the escrow never closed. He said bye-bye to his freedom and I said bye-bye to several thousand dollars. Our cheese definitely got moved and so may yours.

These are just a few examples of some of the difficult circumstances that you are likely to encounter when you are engaging with people whose lives are in transition. You will also be encountering a lot of other agents who are relatively new to the business. Since they are inexperienced, possibly inadequately trained, they can present a challenge to the smooth flow of your business.

I went to a seller's home to present an FHA purchase offer on behalf of my client. FHA loans can cost a seller more than a conventional loan. When I turned to the seller's agent and suggested she present her seller's net proceeds estimate she said, "What?"

I asked again, "Did you prepare a seller's net sheet… ya know, the bottom line?"

"No" she said, "I don't think we've gotten to that part of the training yet." How she got the listing is hard to explain since the seller had no idea how much money he was going to walk away with at closing. When I showed him, he took his home off the market.

From the outside, the real estate business can give the impression that it is not too strenuous. It may not appear to be physically demanding, but being strong and healthy definitely has its advantages since you never know what you will encounter.

Maintaining good health is an important business objective of a personal service business. Without you, there is no business.

If you cannot work, your business will collapse. Also, when people employ you to perform an important function they make judgments about you. Yes, they do. Do you make good decisions in your own life? Do you have the energy to do what needs to be done? Do you have the self-discipline to avoid temptation? When they refer business to you, they will scrutinize you even more closely. They're taking a risk, and unlike a conventional employer, they are under no obligation to hire you or refer business to you, no matter the reason.

The greatest risk to your business is poor health in general, and obesity in particular. As someone building a personal service business, you are in a position of leadership within your community and you have a greater responsibility to be a role model for good health and wellness. Spread the word and your customers will live longer, earn more, and buy more real estate.

America's obesity epidemic is a national health crisis that we simply cannot afford to treat with any conventional medical approach. But, if nothing is done, we will bankrupt the nation and needlessly destroy the lives of people who simply do not know that they have choices. This crisis is the result of ill-informed and misinformed consumers. The very industries that make America fat all have side businesses in drugs, diet products, and related services.

Having said that, I do not believe in dieting as a means to attaining optimum health because it is misfocused and works only for those individuals that incorporate other positive steps in addition to dieting. You cannot deny and deprive your way to a better outcome.

Diets do not work. The word "diet," which should have no connotation at all, has become a negative associated with deprivation. My "diet" consists of all of the fresh spinach, strawberries, nuts, and lean protein I want, and my food looks so delicious I often take pictures while I'm making it and just before I eat.

Check it out on my website.

Here is an important principle by which to build your business: **You can't do a don't.** Instead, you must be proactive. Resolutions all too frequently are little more than a list of things we think we ought not to do. Don't eat that, don't procrastinate, don't waste time, and don't earn less than six figures.

There is a lot of food in real estate. Back in the day it was pretty much only doughnuts, but depending on where you are, some local caravans are like a moving feast. Then there is lunch. All too often it is just agents going to lunch with other agents and eating too much stuff they shouldn't. Not to mention the glass of wine or two.

You are in business. The last people you should be having lunch with are other agents unless you are asking them for referrals. Good luck with that. Lunch is not about you and your stomach, it is about generating referrals. By the time I had figured this out, I had put on about 25 pounds. Get a small salad and pick at it. You only have a few minutes to make your presentation and cement their intention to refer their community, i.e. friends, family, neighbors, and co-workers.

REPEAT POSITIVE AFFIRMATIONS

Many years ago, I printed two affirmations on 3 by 5 cards and taped them on the light above my bed. "I have a slender, well-muscled body," and "I am a wonderful and prolific writer."

Well, at least I have been prolific and I have a slender, well-muscled body; those are the things over which I have control. With writing, as with any skill, if you do it often enough over a long enough period, you cannot help but get good at it. So there is still hope.

Affirmations are present tense expressions as though you had already achieved the desired outcome. Affirmations are like a road map for your subconscious to always propel you in the direction of that which you had affirmed.

EAT HEALTHY

I did not diet; rather I turned to mindful eating and the gym. I did not aim for a certain weight or try to lose 30 pounds. I am 5 foot 7 inches, I went from 165 pounds to 125 pounds, and I kept it off. I have a pair of Levis that I bought in 1992. They have a 31-inch waist, and there is room for a good-sized meal between me and the waistband.

I worked it off and I keep on working because it has many more rewards beyond not having to diet. What I do is avoid prepackaged crap. When you train as hard as I do, you do not want to compromise the effort by depriving your body of what it really needs. The surprise is that when you work your body hard, the foods you should be eating are the ones you crave the most — not gobs of goo and chemical additives.

Processed foods contain ingredients I cannot pronounce. So what? The effects of many of these substances over time are only now coming to light. But, considering the state of our health as a nation since we altered our diet, it is fairly apparent that it cannot be good for you.

Processed foods are not very nutritious. The constant craving experienced by many people who consume large amounts of processed food is a form of deprivation that ultimately contributes to our high obesity rates. The lower the nutritional value, the more the body craves it. It is a human survival system in perfect tune with health and longevity until it is tweaked by symptoms of starvation produced by processed food.

I have no desire for fast food. Although, I used to crave it like everyone else, I am now over it. I know I could eat it if I wanted to, but the very idea is now entirely unappealing. A quarter pounder with cheese and some fries are not going to kill me, but I know that for a couple hours afterward, I'm not going to feel good. What we put into our bodies makes a huge difference in how our bodies perform, and consequently affects our view of life.

When presented with food not in my meal plan, I just ask myself, "Do I really want this?" And sometimes the answer comes back, "Hell, yeah!"

That is the best part; I never feel deprived, and because I eat healthy 90 percent of the time, it really doesn't matter. I subscribe to the smorgasbord theory of eating: if you eat a little of everything, you will fill up before you eat too much of anything.

Changing eating habits is a journey of a lifetime. Many people do not even take the first step because they do not believe that they can succeed. Nevertheless, taking a first step, even a small one, is a reversal in course. Doing nothing is continuing to head in the wrong direction. Dramatically reduce consumption of sugar and its substitutes, such as high fructose corn syrup. The introduction of HFCs into processed foods corresponds exactly with our obesity problem. We consume more sugar per day than our ancestors did during their entire lives. Elementary school class photos from the 40s and 50s demonstrate that the average child's body has gone from ectomorph to mesomorph.

Dr. Roy Wahlford was a pathologist and leading researcher on maximal life expectancy. His research indicated that a diet of no more than 900 calories per day could lead to a life of between 120 and 140 years. Calorie restriction is designed to bring down glucose and insulin levels, reduce body fat, lower levels of growth stimulators, prevent cell loss, decrease inflammation, and create a more youthful physique.

Nine hundred calories borders on starvation, and yet, if living to an old age while remaining healthy is the goal, calorie restriction can further that effort. Sure, you could still get hit by a bus, but that is something that is out of your control. Nine hundred calories is too extreme for most of us, but that does not mean that you cannot take simple, painless steps toward a more thoughtful way of eating. Don't think of it as dieting. It is choosing more wisely, which begins by being better informed.

Because food is everywhere, we tend to take it for granted and often eat without thinking. If you simply think about what you put in your mouth, you will begin the slow but steady journey to a healthier, happier life. Rather than tackling the entire problem at once, just take the first step. After that, it gets easier. There is a synergy that kicks in, if you let it. As you begin to feel better, you will find yourself physically craving healthier food and intellectually eschewing bad choices. And, if you are exercising, you will not want to invest all that time and then put crap into your body.

Most big agra-products that are processed contain high fructose corn syrup. Most soda pop, typically big brands, contains large amounts of high fructose corn syrup, too. Recently, a coroner in Australia blamed a young mother's death on her habit of drinking two gallons of Coke every day. He reported that "her body failed because she had caused chemical changes in her organs." If it will eat rust off of chrome, imagine what Coke does to your digestive system.

Consumers need to become better informed regarding the health consequences of the typical American diet. Not that long ago, we believed that all food was good for you. But, much about the food itself has changed since the 50s. We need to allow ourselves to benefit from the possession of new and better information. That is what a business would do, and you are your business.

KEEP MOVING

Get on the move, and stay on the move. Without movement and resistance, the strength to hang onto the back of someone's pants with one hand will not be available when you need it most.

Just like your business, if it's important, it needs to be planned right into your week, not left to some "spare" time that will never come. If you have any actual spare time, please send it to me; I never have enough.

We now know virtually everything we need to know about what we need to do to not only feel our best, but also to avoid many debilitating and expensive ailments. Move and eat well. That's it. Two powerful forces must be overcome in order to achieve these two simple business objectives: inertia and temptation.

You must therefore decide what is most important to you, building a rewarding real estate business one certain step at a time, or giving in to the temptation to deviate from your plan. Because interacting with people is the single most important aspect of your business, you want to schedule activities where that will occur. Join groups centered on active pursuits.

One of the most interesting and rewarding things I have ever done was a botany course at Palomar College lead by Wayne Armstrong. Hold your laughter for a moment, but the focus of the course was finding and identifying spring wildflowers.

This is excerpted from the course guide:

"Botany 110 is a course in plant identification and ecology. It is

called Botany of Spring Wildflowers. This is a four-unit transferable lecture/lab course in the natural sciences, usually offered on Tuesday evenings with six Saturday field trips. The course involves the use of dissecting microscopes and dichotomous taxonomic keys. Each week during the laboratory session, students must identify several unknown plants by the end of each class period. Field trips will include natural history and ecology of plant communities in San Diego County."

Actually, it was amazing! The class was devoted to identifying plants based upon a microscopic examination of the characteristics of the flower. On Saturday, we went out into the field and hiked the widely varying habitats that create an amazing array of plants in San Diego County. The plants along the coast are nothing like those just a few miles inland.

As a business decision, you might wonder if the time was well spent. Evening and weekend classes have more working adults, so I was learning firsthand about the native plants of San Diego County while hiking outdoors in remote areas with very interesting people.

Additionally, I learned a wealth of information of great value to my clients because I can talk knowledgably about landscaping, native plants, drought tolerance, and the different ecosystems that exist in San Diego's unique range of habitats. The college was in the center of my geographic community, so as I was building my business, I was also learning basic and vital information, having fun, and exercising.

Unlike most agents working in the county, one of my first questions is "What type of climate do you want to live in?" San Diego County runs all the way from the seashore to the desert with snowy mountains in between. This class allowed me to see that.

MAKE A LIST OF EVERYTHING YOU ENJOY DOING

Underline all of those that have people-meeting potential. Now, go back and circle those that are active and will get you moving, and schedule them as you would any work appointment. If you will not invest in your health for business reasons, think about it this way: the greatest gift you can ever give to those you love is vitality and presence in their lives.

Remember, you are starting a business where the odds of success are the same as being selected to Harvard Law School — just seven percent. You cannot afford to leave anything to chance. Just about good enough is a one-way ticket to two part-time jobs with low wages.

When viewed from a business perspective, health is either an asset or a liability. Vitality, energy, optimism, and confidence are clearly assets. Sluggishness, exhaustion, and depression are liabilities. Remember, building a business is a step-by-step process that continually seeks to optimize resources over the course of its life. Minimize weaknesses by maximizing strengths. It is all about building a better you, about focusing on what you can become rather than what you have been.

Schedule everything that is important — day by day, week by week, person by person, step by step, and rep by rep. Have lunch every day with someone you know to make your referral presentation. Do something active with others every day for the purpose of discovering more candidates for lunch. Train and prepare pre-planned meals every day.

Eventually, all of this will become habit; this will be your life. Every day will be relatively the same as yesterday. That is what a good business does. It is consistent in the application of principals that work. The results we get from our endeavors are based

THE AWFUL TRUTH ABOUT CAREERS IN REAL ESTATE AND WHAT TO DO ABOUT IT

on our behavior. Behavior is the by-product of our thoughts. Therefore, getting different results requires a change in thinking, a new mindset, a step outside the box, a paradigm shift.

What should you plan? Fuel and fun. Plan your meals; you owe that to yourself. Plan fun movement with others.

"Stay healthy, my friend."

CHAPTER 15

WHAT TO WEAR

"Nothing you wear is more important than your smile."
—CONNIE STEVENS

Dressing for success in real estate is a little more complicated than dressing for success on Wall Street, unless your sphere of influence happens to work on Wall Street. Therein lies one of the main factors — who is in your sphere of influence, and what do they do?

The next factor is the marketplace itself. Where is your sphere of influence located? What are the people wearing to conduct business? Which leads us to another important consideration; this is business. Unless your sphere of influence is confined to personal trainers and pro athletes, then workout wear is probably not appropriate.

The purpose of your business wardrobe is to convey a sophisticated image that just hints at success, sends an impression of professionalism, and is flattering without being suggestive. The message you want your *costume* to convey is that you are self-aware, savvy, in touch, and capable. You do not want to attract attention because of what you wear; you want it to confirm your professional abilities.

Who do you know and what do they do? Many of my clients were softball players and their friends, co-workers, family, and neighbors. If it was a player on my own team, he would have thought it odd had I showed up wearing a suit. If it were the head of his department at work, I would either wear a suit or a sport coat.

What is unique about your marketplace? Is there waterfront? Is it cold? Are there farms and ranches? I came to real estate from a business marketing background, and I was comfortable in a suit and tie. But, my office was located in Poway, California, which was a distant horse-oriented suburb of San Diego at the time. It took me a while to adjust, but the situation and the people involved became my guide.

In trying to dress the part, men might wind up looking like gigolos with the open collar and the gold medallions or complete slobs spilling out of ill-fitting garments. Most women seem to have a better fashion sense than men, but when women have a fashion fail, it can be more dramatic. Women must also consider the implications of attire that is too revealing.

Does it say you are a strong negotiator? Are other women intimidated or jealous? If you really want to show off, get in great physical condition. It will show right through whatever you wear and it says, "I am a thoughtful, hardworking professional with the energy to get the job done." Real estate is a high-energy business with tremendous highs and lows. Being fit and healthy is one of your business's biggest assets. You cannot afford to be sick.

I worked in men's fashion for a few years so I feel qualified to make specific suggestions for men, but not so much for women. But the general rule still applies; it should be appropriate to the people and circumstances in your community

For both men and women, never wear flip-flops anywhere, ever, except at home. Men, no one wants to see your feet. If you work in a tropical resort community there are other appropriate choices of footwear available for both men and women. There are no excuses for flip-flops.

BASIC WARDROBE FOR MEN

The basics for men should include clothing with value, versatility, and flexibility. A navy blue blazer and charcoal gray slacks with a blue Oxford cloth button-down shirt, red and blue rep stripe tie and black lace-up shoes is a look that can go almost anywhere. However, you may feel a little like a Catholic schoolboy. Add a pair of brown or cordovan slip-on shoes and good quality khaki slacks, ditch the tie, and you are a little more casual, but still business like.

The next addition would be a good quality, well-tailored medium gray suit. For the most conservative look, add a white spread collar shirt and a red tie. The thing about gray is that the possibilities for different colored shirts and ties are almost endless. Purple, pink, French blue and light blue all offer the possibility for creating an entirely different look.

So, we have a gray suit, navy blazer, two pairs of slacks, four shirts, four ties, two pair of shoes and multiple interchangeable pieces. When the funds are available for you to expand your wardrobe, I would add a navy blue vested suit. The shirts and ties you already have will work perfectly.

Next, I would add a gray herringbone sport coat. It too will go with everything you already have, but you could add a nubby-weave tie and you will be ready to go hang out on campus. When it gets chilly, pick up a red V-neck sweater. You can also wear this under the blazer.

Next up, a black or brown suit. A black suit can fulfill the need for something really staid and formal without having to go to a tuxedo. If I had to choose though, I would go with brown. Brown goes great with the blue shirts and ties, as well as giving an opportunity to add tan and brown hues to the wardrobe.

CHAPTER 16

MONEY, MONEY, MONEY

"Once I lived the life of a millionaire, spending my money like I didn't care."
—NOBODY KNOWS YOU WHEN YOU'RE DOWN AND OUT, DEPRESSION-ERA SONG LYRIC.

For more than a century, the goal has been to be a millionaire. From 1955 to 1960, America was fascinated by a CBS television series called "The Millionaire." It told the stories of people who were given one million dollars from a benefactor who insisted they never know him.

The idea isn't about a particular amount of money, but about the amount needed to be free from anxiety. However, a million dollars ain't what it used to be, but then neither is money itself. Today a million dollars is not likely to make much of a change in your life. It is good pay for a year, but a million dollars will not buy a private island, a private jet, or allow for early retirement. It would be a nice cushion, but it will not cause any dramatic change in your life, except that you will probably worry about it all the time. And you should; it's worthless. It can be easily taken from you and most likely will once physical currency is eliminated in favor of digital.

Money and real estate go hand in hand. Money is a tool of your profession. Most people have no understanding whatsoever of how money functions and take it entirely for granted. But, you are in real estate, and you have an obligation to understand money in detail.

In order to build a referral business, you have to have the trust of the people who know you. That requires a high level of competence and a deep understanding of how things work. Therein lies the justification for a chapter on money. Real estate is the answer to the question, "What should I do with my worthless fiat currency?"

The money chapter is important since for the last ten years and the next ten to come, we will be dealing with the fall-out from Wall Street's designed to fail loans.

To better obtain referrals to listings that result from a dying economy, one needs to understand the underlying circumstances. Practitioners serve better if they do not buy into the heavily promoted media victim blaming and believe that the borrowers did it to themselves.

I get more calls about these issues than anything and my workshops are full of real estate agents trying to wrap their heads around this. In my experience, very few people have any idea about money and banking. At least people in real estate should be informed, if only as a sign of competence.

Those who understand the current monetary system, such as those who work in the financial services industry, have for some time, in anticipation of monetary and economic instability, been converting their money to real property. They understand that money is infinite and thus has no value. Real estate is in extremely short supply and it has utility. Its cash value may fluctuate relative to the condition of the economy, but its actual value is reflected in its utility; you can live on it, work on it, or maybe even grow food on it.

My experience with real estate agents is that most haven't a clue about money, so understanding this will give you a further advantage over them as you bring greater value to the consumer. Once you fully understand the monetary system and learn the truth about money, you will never see the world the way you did before. It is akin to being the only survivor of a horrible disaster. Life and time are suddenly way more precious and valuable than a fist full of IOUs. There are essentially two paths one can take in life: the one to a nonexistent place called security or the road to self-fulfillment.

We wrongly believe that wealth will make us feel secure and fulfilled someday while we ache to pursue our true purpose of self-development in the moment. Security is an illusion; one that has been further perpetuated by our willingness to swap our individual liberties in exchange for a promise of safety from a boogey man who does not exist. No amount of money can protect one from the loss of a loved one, illness, aging or death. Do not get me wrong; I am not an advocate for poverty. I am an advocate of being rich in spirit, gratitude, purpose, and fulfillment, and only in self-discovery and personal development can those things be had.

I do not buy lottery tickets because I do not want to waste what I might need later. But, the real reason is that I want to see what I can accomplish if I keep on working to get better, be better, and serve better.

Once you comprehend money, you will feel liberated, and indeed you have been. Once you understand money you will realize that the only true source of wealth is that which you can attain through abilities you have acquired and mastered. When you build a business to make a profit, the business has no foundation. If you build a business to create customers, you will always make a profit. Having said that, you will still need to do some budgeting and money management for your business.

What I am about to share with you may at first seem preposterous, but I assure you that it is completely factual and much has been written on the topic. In that regard, this is not intended to be comprehensive or complete. I am not an expert on the topic, just a stunned researcher trying to present the gist of the thing to a layperson.

THE MODERN GLOBAL MONETARY FARCE

In order to understand the state of the modern monetary system, it is necessary to understand the meaning of a few common terms, as well as overcome false perceptions. Among the important terms are: The Federal Reserve Bank, Fiat Currency, and Fractional Reserve Banking.

Let's start with a few little known facts to dispel your false perception of money.

Money is debt

Without debt there would be no money. If everyone paid back his or her debt, there would be no money in circulation. As I am writing this, we have what is known as a "debt-based" monetary system, which we are stuck with for the moment. Debt, taken on for the right purposes, can be a very positive thing under the right circumstances. Debt taken on for the purpose of leverage to acquire appreciating assets or future cash flows, which would be sufficient to retire the debt in a reasonable amount of time, would constitute a responsible use of debt. Depreciating assets and consumables, on the other hand should be purchased with revenues, not debt.

Wouldn't it be better to pay cash for everything including real estate and have no debt? Yes! But that takes a lot of advance planning considering you would need to select a wealthy family to be born into. Real estate is expensive and few people would be able to save enough in their lifetime to afford it. That is when leverage is good. Businesses require capital for startup and expansion, and usually have little choice but to borrow.

You have no money in the bank

You have a credit. The money you think you have has never even been printed. If everyone went to the bank to get their money, the money would run out quickly and most would get nothing more than a lecture about the meaning of all of that fine print in the paperwork you signed when you opened your account.

There is no money

There is no money, just accountants, lawyers, and entries in ledgers.

Oh, there is a little bit of it floating around to keep things moving, but that's just for show, and there is a movement afoot to abolish the use of physical currency altogether. They want you to pay with your smartphone and become part of the virtual money farce.

According to the Federal Reserve, there was only $1.1 trillion in U.S. currency in circulation as of June 20, 2012. As of Sept. 26, 2012, there was $1.13 trillion. That is anything but a dramatic increase in the money in circulation. In fact it is a disturbingly small number when compared to the $1,000 trillion invested in "derivatives," which have no value of their own but derive it from something else.

The money supply fluctuates over the course of the year as banks see more demand for cash for gift shopping and year-end vacations. There are actually times when banks have excess cash that they send back to the Treasury. So much for an economy awash in recently printed money.

It is the banks themselves who determine how much cash they need as seasonal fluctuations occur. Right now, there is an extraordinary demand for American currency in Europe as those who see the writing on the wall seek a safer haven than the Euro. Consequently, as much as two-thirds of the $1.13 trillion is held overseas. That means that there is only about $400 billion in actual money propping up a government that is $19 trillion in debt.

Meanwhile, Jamie Dimon, CEO of JPMorgan Chase, claims that Chase has $1.3 trillion in cash deposits. Other banks make similar claims, none of which can be true. Each of the big banks would hold more cash than the treasury actually printed. Money is more of an accounting trick, and the entire monetary system is based on accounting tricks.

Most people alive today were born into this system. We take it for granted. We do not teach it in school. You think you know what money is; it seems pretty simple. It is a method of storing value; it is a means of exchange that facilitates easier commerce between traders of goods and services. Bankers broker the exchanges between them, and we never think about how it all works.

About three percent of our money originates from the treasury, not the Fed as we are often misdirected to believe, in the form of notes and coins. The rest is digital and created by private banks, out of nothing, when they issue loans. It is just virtual money, not actual money.

Banks create virtual money when someone borrows it

When we go to a bank to take out a loan, the bank does not lend its own money or that of its depositors, they use new loans to make up money that did not previously exist. Banks create the amount borrowed but not the interest to be paid on that amount. The result is that there is now more debt than there is money. The unfortunate aspect of this scheme is that there must be an ever-increasing amount of lending to cover the debt plus interest while maintaining the amount of money in circulation. See the problem? The very system we are part of requires more and more debt in order to function.

In a debt-based monetary system, only when money is borrowed does it come into existence. Did you get that? Those of you who already know this know the futility of trying to explain it to someone. It goes completely contrary to everything we thought we knew about banking and money.

That is why banks want all of us to borrow. It is not the goods we made and bought that got us our "thriving" economy. Those SUVs, McMansions, the J Crew fashions, and the $29 banana-walnut-caramel frappe with a triple shot were not responsible either. It was the money that was created when we borrowed to buy them and used our credit cards.

Students graduating with large loans acquired to train them for jobs that do not exist, well, they were just another target of subprime loans designed to never be repaid. Subprime auto loans and preprinted checks flooding mailboxes were also part of the great debt pig-out. The monetary system must create debt in order to survive. That means that more debt needs to be created every year in excess of the debt, as well as the interest from the prior year.

Not only can our debt never be paid off, but if it were, the system would collapse. But never mind that, we are well beyond that at the other end of the spectrum. That is why there is way more debt globally than can be sustained.

If debts were paid off, the money supply would shrink. Even if we pay off our debts, collectively we are in debt forever, paying interest to the banks.

Is it any wonder then that very few people now own almost everything? This monetary system means governments do not issue the money they spend, but go into debt to private banks that "lend" money they simply create. Obviously, this system is doomed to failure as its essential structure is that of a Ponzi scheme.

FIAT CURRENCY

What little money actually exists has no greater value than cut up pieces of Piggly Wiggly grocery bags.

"Fiat" is a Latin word that roughly translates into "because I say so." Thus, a dollar is worth a dollar because Uncle Sam says so. The dollar is backed by the "full faith and credit" of the United States government. In other words, absolutely nothing at all. That is it; money backed by nothing more than the hollow promise of a bankrupt government. Are you laughing yet?

Nothing to worry about unless you have a government that proves at every turn that it is not to be trusted, and of whom it is well understood on the global front is completely and unequivocally tapped out. And remember, the U.S. already defaulted the dollar on August 15, 1971, when Richard Nixon appeared on television and told the world that we were not going to honor our obligation to redeem the paper for gold. On that day, nations that were holding U.S. dollars, because they believed they really were gold, were left with paper and promises.

Since that day, we have had to retain our position as the world's reserve currency by force; hence, all of the war-mongering. But, as I write this, we appear to be losing the battle and other currencies are gaining acceptance.

FRACTIONAL RESERVE BANKING

Every dollar borrowed is worth $10 to the bank

I am not making this up. It is what banking is *really* all about — fractional reserve banking. You have heard the term before, but have you actually considered the implications? The banks only have a <u>fraction</u> of depositor's money; just a small float to cover daily business.

Once you deposit your money, it belongs to the bank, not you. That old attitude of "it's my money and I'll withdraw it all if I want to" is false. The agreement you signed when you opened your account says you are entitled to a credit in the institution.

The Federal Reserve

Despite the title, it is not a federal agency or a bank, and it does not reserve anything. It is a private corporation that has taken control of our monetary system. Really!

Too harsh? Why is Wall Street an island of prosperity in a global sea of poverty?

The first thing we must do is clear our mind of false information perpetrated by the owners of the Federal Reserve. If you listen to corporate-owned media you have probably heard that the Fed has been printing a lot of money. If, as they say, the Fed has been printing money, wouldn't there be more money for people to spend, to build things, to create jobs, and pay taxes? Of course there would.

The Fed more closely resembles a gigantic money laundering mechanism that transfers future dollars to the global elite. The Fed does not print anything; it simply hands-out interest free virtual money to banks, buys toxic assets from banks, and puts the loss on the American tax payer. If someone would buy all

MONEY, MONEY, MONEY

of your phony investment pools, why would you stop creating them?

The Treasury is the actual printer of the money, although they have not been printing any either. Lately, the bills I have been getting are in their final stage of utility — wrinkly, faded, soiled, and tattered — like my wardrobe. I even had to tape one at the hinge to keep it from splitting in two.

If there really were more money being put into circulation, you would feel it. I am not feeling it; just the opposite. In the words of Simply Red front-man, Mick Hucknall, "money's too tight to mention."

The Federal Reserve loans banks money at zero percent, ZIRP (Zero Interest Rate Program) so the banks can use the interest free money to buy Treasury Bonds that pay them 3.5 percent interest. The Federal Reserve is considering NIRP (Negative Interest Rate Program), wherein depositors would pay interest to the banks. Fearing that depositors would withdraw all their money, cash would be replaced with digital currency and those few printed dollars.

Where does the Federal Reserve get the money they loan the banks at zero percent? They make it up. Who pays the interest on the treasuries the banks buy with the phony money created for them by the Federal Reserve Bank? The American taxpayer. I told you it was hard to believe.

Let's pause for a moment and reflect on the above.

A private corporation makes up dollars to essentially give to banks guaranteeing them enormous risk free, tax payer-funded profits. For all of the money being pumped through the system, it creates not one job nor does it build a house or a microchip, and the value is steadily reduced as the supply continues to grow.

So there it is — the big banksta business plan in a nutshell. A direct tax payer-funded gift to the bonus babies of Wall Street. They call that capitalism and the free market economy; I call it corporate welfare and organized crime.

But, they couldn't stop there. When you can just go to the Fed window and get all of the taxpayer funded cash you can carry, where's the fun? Where's the challenge?

Shadow banking

Some have referred to a "shadow banking system." These financial intermediaries avoid all of the regulation in the traditional banking system and are subject to no oversight. Capitalism and a free market economy are an illusion. The problem is that only about one out of a thousand people actually know anything about banking.

I was once one of you. I thought banking was sort of obvious and mundane. People need a place to keep their money. Innovation needs capital to create productivity. Back in the day, it was all pretty local and that was about it. Bankers were still the richest guys in town and anyone who ever played Monopoly knows that you want to be the bank.

Those who really understand banking do not talk about it in public. They are either part of the secret society or they have learned that, in discussions of the economy, if one actually knows how the banking system works and attempts to illuminate others, it will earn them a reputation for being odd. Knowing the secrets of banking is like seeing a UFO. Who would ever believe you?

That is part of the problem. Released from our shackles, we can see that the shadows on the wall are not reality, but they are all we have ever known. I used to think I was pretty savvy, but, I am just country-boy smart, not felonious smart. I had

MONEY, MONEY, MONEY

no idea what was going on. None. Even when I had been to the bottom of the rabbit hole, I was stunned and dumbfounded for six months. It was just so hard to believe.

And then, where do you even begin to tell the story? Let's take the simplest part first.

The "banks" that I am referring to are not really banks in the traditional sense; they are more akin to a cartel. They are called "investment banks," but financial intermediary would be a better definition. Among the largest are Bank of America, Citibank, Deutsche Bank, Goldman Sachs, JPMorgan Chase, UBS, and Wells Fargo.

Just over 100 years ago, seeing an opportunity, wealthy individuals created "Central Banks." For now, we will skip the history of how this came about — believe me you are not ready for that. More recently, the Financial Services Modernization Act of 1999 (also known as the Gramm-Leach-Bliley Act) and the Commodity Futures Modernization Act of 2000 brought home the pork bellies for the banks.

What if, and this is where I lose most people, so stay with me, what if the real goal all along has been a global economic collapse? Why would they want that to happen? Because they own massive credit-default swaps that pay them for virtually every credit failure imaginable.

"At their most basic level, innovations like the ones that triggered the global collapse — credit-default swaps and collateralized debt obligations — were employed for the primary purpose of synthesizing out of thin air those revenue flows that our dying industrial economy was no longer pumping into the financial blood stream," said Matt Taibbi in his article "Wall Street's Naked Swindle" published in Rolling Stone.

Never mind the CDOs and the MBS and the derivatives all

being completely worthless, the money supposedly behind them is actually worthless. Oh, that's right, it is insured by the FDIC; silly me, why was I worrying? I am sure they will be able to get the tens of trillions of dollars somewhere.

MASSIVE MORTGAGED-BACKED SECURITIES FRAUD

The mortgage bonds sold by banks to investors are a fraud in progress. The bonds are backed by nothing at all. They were never properly securitized, the values are fiction, and the same mortgages are pledged to multiple pools.

Once you start breaking the law to make money, it would be a bad business decision to stop. Viewed in that context, one must realize that these people will do whatever they can get away with, and they have been allowed to get away with almost everything.

The recently signed settlements and consent decrees are another example of bank defiance of the law in that they continue to employ the same unlawful practices that they agreed to cease. It has been eight years since I wrote my first column suggesting that mortgage servicers were foreclosing on homeowners who were not in breach of their agreements. At that time, I knew nothing of debt securitization, credit default swaps, or derivatives. My earliest investigations led quickly to one important aspect of all of this, and in September of 2009, I wrote, "Sixty Million Mortgages May Have Fatal Flaws," one of the earliest articles exposing the murky MERS connection and the looming title problems. As amazing as that is, that was not the story, just a side bar. But, it raised the question of the real reason for MERS existence.

Mortgages designed by risk experts to increase defaults to record levels

The NINA loan — no income, no assets. Who would ever think of such a thing? Not the borrower.

Now we know that Wall Street had designed a number of new mortgage products containing features that, based on their studies of mortgage risk, would lead to dramatically higher default rates than those of past mortgages. You read that right; they studied the risks associated with mortgage lending and wove into these new loans the very seeds of default. For decades, the foreclosure rate for residential mortgages hovered under 0.5 percent.

According to a recent report from the Mortgage Bankers Association, "The combined percentage of loans in foreclosure or at least one payment past due was 12.63 percent on a non-seasonally adjusted basis."

What about the performance of those new and improved mortgage loans designed by risk actuaries for Wall Street securitization? How are those performing? Well, if we were in the business of minimizing risk, at minimum we might want to hire some better actuaries. The delinquency and foreclosure rates are up astronomically for the newly improved mortgages. The delinquency rate was 19.67 percent for subprime fixed-rate loans and 22.4 percent for subprime adjustable-rate loans. The foreclosure rate for subprime ARM loans was 22.17 percent. Either those actuaries are chimpanzees or the loans are performing even better than expected. They were designed to be unsustainable. Now we know why. They bought insurance on these products that paid them huge bonuses if the defaults occurred.

I will concede that there are those of you out there who know way more about this than I do, and you are probably itching to set me straight on a thing or two, but the outcomes of bank practices speak for themselves. Cities filing for bankruptcy, states facing bankruptcy, nations on the brink of collapse, global unemployment, austerity, fraudclosures, food stamp use, and rising levels of poverty are happening right here. Who gets the credit for that?

The next time someone says that we need the banks because they are the innovators who create jobs and fuel the economy, tell them that they are really parasites sucking the very marrow out of humanity. Because that is what banks really do.

UNDERSTANDING THE ECONOMY

It looks amazingly real, but the economy is as phony as a James Cameron movie set. Its many moving parts exist only for the purpose of creating the illusion of positive economic activity. When you go behind the scenes, it is evident that those things that seem so real are merely props held up plywood. Lashed together with synthetic credit default obligations, bankruptcy remote special purpose vehicles, and leveraged beyond reason, the set appears massive and foreboding from the front. But, when you go behind the façade, it is apparent that the whole thing is on the very verge of collapse. Never mind, it was engineered to collapse when the show is over. But, wait! This is a disaster movie, so the set is actually rigged to explode.

The economy is a fantasy woven of greed and collusion, and it is allowing a handful of already wealthy people to concentrate all of the wealth and power into their hands while destroying everyone and everything else. The economy reflects the efficiency of the distribution of goods and services. By simply looking around, one can tell how well the economy around them is functioning.

Recently, I happened upon a rather esoteric online debate about whether or not the economy is real. One argument was

MONEY, MONEY, MONEY

that it exists; therefore, it must be real. A movie is real, but its components are created, and the story line may be fiction. That is the case with the economy; it is real, but it is not at all what it appears to be.

What do we mean when we say "the economy"? What is it? What is the difference between a good economy and a bad one? There is an old line that when your neighbor loses his job, it is a recession, but when you lose your job, it is a depression. The economy is not so much a thing but a reflection, more symptom than cause. It is a measure of how effectively we turn inputs into outputs. The best economy for all parties is generally thought to be one that distributes goods and services the most efficiently. In theory, improving the efficiencies with which we distribute goods and services within a community should have a positive effect on everyone.

Prior to profit driven globalization, economies were primarily local and served to provide for basic needs. The farmer grows a crop of carrots and sells it to the general store. The farmer buys a hoe, some seeds, and three yards of gingham. It is a well-known fact that farmers have daughters. Did you hear the one about…?

The storeowner orders more goods, makes a donation to the church, and orders a shot of red eye at the honky-tonk. But, the storeowner cannot just pay in carrots. A common means of exchange is essential to a fully functioning economy, and money became the solution.

In a sense, there are two economies: the one described by economists, politicians, and a lapdog media, and the one that more and more middle class Americans are living in — the real world. One wonders: why the disconnect?

Americans' wages have been steadily declining in the face of rising prices, unemployment is high, the average workweek is 33 hours, millions are losing their homes, and Wall Street CEOs earn huge bonuses for deliberately stealing our prosperity. As more and more capital is concentrated into the hands of a few, it is unlikely we will see any improvement.

We have hit the wall. With wages flattening, we cannot borrow anymore. No more borrowing means no more made up money. So, the first consequence has occurred as consumers discover the inevitable and unavoidable feature of debt-based money; without endless borrowing, it cannot be sustained. Endless borrowing is a physical impossibility. Without consumer spending, jobs disappear and fewer taxes are collected to pay both the debt and expenses.

The standard measure of the economy is the National Income and Product Accounts (NIPAs) produced by the Bureau of Economic Analysis (BEA). According to the BEA, "The NIPAs are a set of economic accounts that provide information on the value and composition of output produced in the United States during a given period and on the distribution and uses of the income generated by that production."

We often hear references to the Gross Domestic Product, or GDP, which is featured in the NIPAs. GDP is not the only component. GDP measures the value of the goods and services produced by the U.S. economy in a given time period. Who uses the GDP? Well, Wall Street for one and the Federal Reserve to formulate monetary policy. The White House and Congress use the GDP to prepare the federal budget. The GDP is the measure of the total of all the money spent during a given period to determine the direction and pace of production. If this period shows an increase over the prior period, we are presumed to have a good economy.

But is it accurate? Heck no! These books are as cooked as our collective gooses.

It is what they do not tell you. They do not tell you that the GDP counts liabilities as assets, just like Wall Street. They do not tell you that a cancer patient in their last year of life boosts the GDP more than a family of four who stays home and has dinner together. Going out and eating fast food, wasting gas, and the associated health problems are all good for the GDP.

One thing the GDP does not do is measure waste; it only measures growth of selected outputs. It was not really developed as an economic tool, but as a way of identifying, locating, and enumerating what could be taxed. What began as a sort of property census has become the accepted measure of our economy.

People talk about the economy with the same sort of resolute helplessness they express toward the weather. But, economies are man-made, and despite the almost patriotic assertion otherwise, ours is not a free one. If we have learned anything over the last 10 years, is that the entire system has been hijacked by counterfeiters. Since economies apparently always function to the benefit of the major stakes holders, we can only assume that there is a great deal of cooperation among these entities in order to influence the performance of economies in ways that benefit them. This other economy makes nothing. It simply gobbles up the output and feeds off the real economy.

Governments around the world are now headed where consumers went first — into default. Since the value of everything on the planet is estimated to be about $165 trillion, it raises an interesting question: If a derivative is an investment that has no value of its own, and thereby derives its value from some other asset, and the value of all of those other assets is a mere 25 percent of the total notional value of derivatives, does that mean that everything on the planet is leveraged four to one? These nonexistent dollars are the profits on which shares are valued and bonuses are based.

VIRTUAL MONEY

I always thought the word "avatar" had some sort of mystical meaning, but the first time I recall someone actually using the word "avatar" was several years ago. IBM ran a television commercial in which a character with chin whiskers creates an avatar of himself, authentic down to the billy-goat beard, living on a virtual island on his IBM computer. The other character asks the point of an avatar, and when the bearded dude says, *"To make money"* the other character asks, *"Are you making any money on your island?"* The bearded dude responds with, *"Real money or virtual money?"*

Virtual money? Well, why not? Like a derivative? A thing whose value is not its own, but based on something else. Like an avatar. What about your money? Is it actual money or virtual money?

Obviously, no one (until recently) would accept money if it were not backed by something of value and somehow guaranteed as to its acceptance and redeemability. During those periods when the U.S. was on the gold standard, real assets backed up the paper.

Obviously, that limited the amount of currency in circulation, which further served to protect the value against inflation. Fiat money only works as long as everyone plays along with the naked emperor.

But, wouldn't you just know it, other countries are turning against us and the U.S. dollar. That is really what these endless wars are all about. Oil producing countries have no faith in the U.S. dollar, and you probably should not either.

China is making its move to dethrone the U.S. dollar as the world's reserve currency, a move that is no longer confined to

Asia. At the end of May 2015, China and Japan, China's largest trading partner, agreed to trade directly in each other's currencies paving the way for both the Chinese yuan and the Japanese yen to rise to the status of the world's reserve currency. They are building a firewall to shield themselves from the collapse of economies being dragged down by toxic assets.

The value of the dollar is propped up by nothing more than the hope that a lot of unemployed American's will find jobs, buy things, and pay taxes to whittle down the $19 trillion. But the questions remain, "jobs doing what and for whom?"

Greece, Ireland, Spain, Italy, and Portugal all used to have their own currencies, but now that they are part of the Eurozone, they are being made the patsies for the banks' theft of trillions of dollars that never existed. The idea of a centralized Europe was a bankstas dream. Soon, the only country left standing will be a bloodied and bruised Germany. World War II finally ends — not with a bang, but with a whimper.

No wonder people think international financing is complicated; it defies both logic and explanation. Until they finally figure out why they do not understand it — it is all made up.

THE ABOLISHMENT OF CASH

Have you noticed the persistent messaging that we should all be paying with our smartphones, not cash? You may have also noticed that they are practically giving away smartphones. I believe that they will soon eliminate actual money and replace it with digital entries in a mandatory account.

The Federal Reserve Bank has been threatening for most of the year that next month... next month... next month they will stop the ridiculous policy of giving banks money at zero interest, (ZIRP). I do not believe they will; in fact, I think they plan to go to negative interest (NIRP) even if they do raise rates slightly at first. I think it is just a question of whether there will be one head-fake or two.

The Fed is between a rock and a hard place. All of the quantitative easing has done nothing but embolden and grossly enrich the banking sector. Now the plan is to drop the rate below zero and charge depositors to keep their money in the banks. However, most would withdraw their money and put it in the mattress and earn zero percent rather than pay one percent.

The economy is not recovering, wages are falling, part-time food service jobs have replaced manufacturing jobs, and almost 100 million Americans who could be productive are out of the workforce because there are no jobs, since even working consumers have no money to spend.

The only thing left is to ban cash. It will be made to sound like a really good idea. I can just hear it now: "Cash is barbaric," said someone deeply entrenched in the one percent.

"That would cut down on crime," chimed in another. "Robbing a bank or one of us would be pointless if there were none of that awful, icky cash to be gotten."

"Well, it is only drug dealers and criminals who take advantage of the system who use cash, I use my debit card," added another.

"Yes, of course, among respectable people it is all debit card nowadays."

"I pay everything with my smartphone."

That sounds like a real convenience as long as you have blind faith that your "money" won't be typed into someone else's account, or worse. Remember that the same people who mess

MONEY, MONEY, MONEY

up your phone and cable bills are the same people who will determine how much virtual money you have. What could possibly go wrong?

Smartphones are often essentially free. Now they will be replaced every year. It is a leash; it knows where you are, where you have been, where you are going, who you are, what you think, and how much digital currency you have. The announcement will seem almost innocuous. Effective on a certain date, maybe 90 days, government at all levels will cease to accept any cash but electronic payments only. Anyone who has cash will have 90 days to have it digitized after which it will be declared worthless and illegal with the same penalties that apply to counterfeiting.

In order to prevent riots, all cash exchanged for digital credits at the bank will be paid at the rate of two to one. One dollar of cash for two dollars in your digital account. Whether they offer a 20 percent premium or a 100 percent premium makes no difference since it is all made up.

Since you cannot horde it and you have to pay one percent to the bank to keep it, that digital currency would provide an immediate spark to the economy as people have no choice but to spend it before it declines in value. Then they will play the patriot card and tell us that hoarding cash is un-American in that it is responsible for the economy's failure to recover from the recession while fueling terrorism and crime.

It is not so much that I am sure that it is coming, it is more that I do not see any way it can be avoided. But, what the hell, it's only money, right?

CHAPTER 17

EACH AND EVERY DAY, BETTER IN EVERY WAY

"There is nothing noble in being superior to your fellow man; true nobility is being superior to your former self."
—ERNEST HEMINGWAY

Life is what you make it. And, what you make it depends largely upon what you make of yourself. Of course, you do not have control over everything, and sometimes making the best of things is the only option available. However, the ability to make the best of your circumstances is also a valuable asset that serves well the travelers on the journey of a lifetime.

Just like your clients, you will also experience predictable major life events that will alter the course and circumstances of your life. How you respond will determine the quality of your life. Every setback can be a springboard. Every failure is another vital piece of greater future success. It all depends on you and your attitude.

Life is not supposed to be easy; it is supposed to be challenging if you are doing it right. It will not be easy if you are setting new goals to expand beyond your current limitations. Life has not been easy for me because I keep trying to do difficult things in competitive environments. And, I too have had predictable life events.

We are here to grow, not necessarily to have all of our wishes granted. We are here to strive and struggle; to overcome obstacles external and internal. It is not about "happy ever after," it is about being happy right now doing what you are doing — stretching, striving, and growing. It took me a while to figure that out, and some people never get it at all. I came to a point where I realized that the only way that I was going to have any shot at success in life was to build a much better me than what I was.

Getting better to serve others better is not just the successful philosophy behind building a personal services business, it is also a very satisfying way to spend one's life. To a certain extent I believe that continual self-improvement is vital to longevity. Nature seems to recycle those things that are no longer growing.

Anyone can succeed in this business, and yet almost no one does. You can do this. You can succeed in building a rewarding business if you have the right temperament and are willing to work. No one can stop you but you.

One of my editors asked me if I didn't think that the title of the book should be *Building a Rewarding and **Profitable** Real Estate Business.*

I reminded her of the words of Peter Drucker who stressed, "The purpose of a Business is to create a customer." Profit is a calculation; it is the adjusted cash flow from business revenues. As such, it is not something that can be aimed at. Budgets are created to determine **what** needs to be done with whatever resources are available. Working backward, one can determine how much of **"what"** needs to get done in order to meet budget expectations. That **"what"** is the target, the real goal. How many people will you meet doing things you enjoy doing? That is a goal. How many will you meet with to discuss referrals?

The three most important words in the title are **build, rewarding** and **business. Build a better you and you will attract all you need.**

Rather than aiming at dollars, aim at listings. Set a target for the number of listings you intend to carry in your portfolio and concentrate on that. If you make one new friend every day, have one referral meeting every day, have one well-planned open house per week, see 50 new properties a week, study real estate two hours a day, exercise 90 minutes every day, write, research and practice presentations, you will build a rewarding business.

If you are hoping to get lucky and coast on what you are, you will be among that vast sea of people who come to real estate thinking, "How hard can it be?" Rising above the competition requires perseverance and a willingness to work to get better.

NEVER LOOK BACK AND WONDER WHAT MIGHT HAVE BEEN

One of the men who made a great difference in my life and to whom I will always be grateful was a man who taught me what it means to "go all in." When you aspire to great challenges, commitment is a vital quality. Many people never really make that commitment, and yet, it is commonly known that one cannot steal second base while keeping one's foot on first.

Many people only commit when they can clearly see that they will succeed. Where I come from they say that when it comes to breakfast "the chicken is involved but the pig is committed." Commitment is the very core of character; without it inevitable setbacks become insurmountable barriers. Sometimes a man or woman's true character begins to emerge only after they have come to the realization that God has given them **almost** everything they needed to be great. Malcolm Gladwell has written an extraordinary book, *Outliers: The Story of Success*, which analyzes the circumstances under which people achieve great success. He points out that, while many believe that it is the byproduct of intelligence and ambition, the true story of success is very different; an extraordinary set of circumstances must occur for one to experience great success. Virtually all highly successful people benefited from nurturing, exclusive education, and birth timing. Each generation's most successful men were born within a few years of each other.

Timing is everything. The first mass-media pop star to send throngs of women into hysterics was a crooner with a voice so thin, wavering, and weak that when he performed in public, he had to sing through a megaphone to be heard. However, the expanding medium of radio was all about intimacy, which worked out perfectly and made him one of the biggest stars of his era. His talent was mediocre at best, but his timing was impeccable; not too soon, not too late, just right.

It is not likely that if Rudy Vallee came along today that he would be the superstar that he was in 1930. Who needs a crooner with a megaphone when you have Dr. Dre and Bose?

The question is if Rudy Vallee came along today, would he have put everything he had into a novelty act that would never get him beyond Indian gaming casinos? We know all the stories about the winners, the champions, the few that advance to the pinnacle of their endeavor. But, we do not have too many stories about those who overcome obstacles to compete and excel in second tier venues gaining neither fame nor fortune. What happens to all of those minor-leaguers who came and went, or old wannabees unwilling to fade away?

It is said that a musician is someone who loads $5,000 worth of equipment into a $500 car to drive 100 miles to play a $50 gig. For the vast majority of musicians, a day job is a requirement, and those who can eke out a living slave away in almost total obscurity their entire lives. Many are brilliant musicians who will never see the limelight.

Having had a brush with the theater along my way, I see that beyond the mega stars of Hollywood is an army of "starving" actors wonderfully delivering their lines to audiences of a few dozen people, night after night and twice on Sunday.

Most performers, musicians, athletes, and actors never get beyond their relative "minor leagues." There is a fine line between never giving up and not knowing when to quit. The former is a highly prized quality and the latter is a flaw that can be fatal. I never have been able to figure that one out. Based on my experience, it seems as though doing something is better than doing nothing. I feel it is better to err on the side of proactivity as opposed to defaulting. Everything I have ever attempted I did with the attitude that I would not quit until someone or something stopped me. And I have been stopped, but not before I gave it everything I had. Ross Perot once remarked that most people give up when they are at the one-yard line. I have seen that so often that giving up on anything just is not easy for me. There is so much evidence that just one more try makes all of the difference.

This is the story about a boy from Greybull, Wyoming who went on to be one of the greatest football players of the 1970s that you never heard of unless you have been a 40-year fan of Canadian Football.

Tom Wilkinson was born in Iowa in 1943, and moved to Greybull, Wyoming in 1945. He was a star high school athlete, excelling in both football as a quarterback and baseball as a pitcher. Tom was drafted right out of high school to play baseball. He talked it over with his father who told him that a college education would always have greater value, and together they agreed that Tom would postpone his baseball career until he had completed his education.

Tom attended the University of Wyoming on a football scholarship, lettered three straight years, and set school passing records. In 1966, he began his professional football career when

EACH AND EVERY DAY, BETTER IN EVERY WAY

the Toronto Rifles of the Continental Football League signed him. The Rifles were part of a minor league organization. His pay would be $200 per game. Welcome to professional sports.

Tom drove from Wyoming to Toronto and checked into the hotel on Queen Street that the team had arranged for him. His first moment of doubt struck him as he walked into the lobby and saw a half a dozen guys who were all taller than 6 feet 5 inches. Stunned by what he had seen he called the Rifles coach, Leo Cahill, and asked how the team thought he could compete against players who were so much larger than he. The coach laughed, and Tom was relieved when he discovered that the Detroit Pistons basketball team was in town for an exhibition game and the players were staying at the same hotel.

Canadian football is very similar to the NFL game except that there are three downs to gain 10 yards as opposed to four, and the field is 10 yards wider and longer than an American football field, so it favors the passing game. Doug Flutie was extremely successful in Canada because the game better suited his skill set.

In 1966, Tom passed for 18 touchdowns to earn league Rookie-of-the-Year honors. He played a total of 16 games for the Rifles in 1966 and 1967, throwing the ball 287 times for 141 completions, 1,952 yards, and 11 interceptions. Tom was off to a promising start as a professional football player, but all that ended suddenly with the financial failure of the Continental League. The Rifles played their third and final game of 1967 on Sept. 16.

A lot of players' careers just came to an end that day, but Tom got another chance. The coach of the Rifles, Leo Cahill, had been hired by the Canadian Football League's Toronto Argonauts, and Tom went back to Toronto as a backup quarterback where he would play four seasons. He saw limited action in his first two years, but Tom had a break-out season in 1969, throwing for 2,331 yards and a 56.4 percent completion percentage in nine games.

Despite that performance, Tom was sent back to the bench in 1970, although still got enough playing time to throw for 1272 yards. In 1971, Tom was traded to the British Columbia Lions where he played just one game and was released prior to the start of the 1972 season.

That might have been it. Six seasons of professional football is actually a pretty long career considering that the average is three. But, life is funny. You never really know what is in store for you. You do the best you can today, and the future is what the future is. As Frank Sinatra sang, "you're riding high in April/ Shot down in May." Then one day the phone rang, and it was the Edmonton Eskimos inviting Tom to training camp.

He played well enough in the remaining pre-season games to make the team as a backup, but by season's end he was their top passer with 2,475 yards in which he completed 177 out of 268 pass attempts. In 1973, he led the team to the Canadian equivalent of the Super Bowl, the Grey Cup, where they lost to the Ottawa Rough Riders. The following year he took the Eskimos back to the Grey Cup where they were defeated again, this time by the Montreal Alouettes.

And then, in 1975, it all came together, and in addition to winning the Grey Cup, Tom was named the Most Valuable Player in the league. It was an especially sweet triumph after disappointing losses in the championship games in 1973 and 1974. In 1976, the team came up one game short of making it back to the Grey Cup losing in the conference final.

By the time I met Tom, he had been with the Rifles, the Toronto Argonauts, traded to the British Colombia Lions, released, signed by Edmonton as a backup, become the starter and won a Grey Cup, was the MVP of the League, and came up just short of another Grey Cup appearance.

EACH AND EVERY DAY, BETTER IN EVERY WAY

I was running the promotion department for a newspaper in Edmonton, Alberta. I was the party guy, the schmoozer, the straw that stirred the drink, and it was my job to make people want to buy the newspaper by creating events and opportunities with entertainment, celebrities, athletes, and local luminaries.

The first time I met Tom I was astonished to realize that he was closer to 5 feet 9 inches then 5 feet 11 inches as was listed on the team roster. Although the roster had him weighing 195 pounds, he had to be at least 215 pounds. He was short and fat with a noticeable potbelly, and if it were not for the fact that his shoulders were abnormally wide for a man of his stature, he would have been pear-shaped. He had earned the nickname "The Dwarf."

His general appearance more accurately suggested Quasimodo than a quarterback. He was stocky, scruffy headed, and gravelly-voiced like Andy Devine, but he was also humble and considerate. He did not swear and unlike a lot of other players, he was not a heavy drinker. He switched from cigarettes to chaw and always went around with a cup to spit in.

In 1977, Tom Wilkinson faced yet another turning point in his career. He was overweight, out of shape, and 34-years-old with 10 seasons behind him. In 1977, he ruptured the bursa sac in his throwing elbow and his game had been slowly declining. The media began to run stories about the end of his career, calling him "washed up."

Although, he made it back to the Grey Cup, that did nothing to deter speculation about his future with the team. It was a horrible game played in miserable weather. The game was played in Montreal's Olympic Stadium on Sunday, Nov. 27. I flew in on Friday with a low-grade fever hoping for the best. By Saturday, I was looking for an emergency clinic.

It snowed, partially melted, and snowed some more. The temperature was minus 10 degrees Celsius (about 15 F) throughout the game, which could only be described as a bitter and humiliating defeat, 41-6.

It was an exercise in utter futility as most of the field was covered in sheer ice, and the players were falling down all over the field. For a passing game like Tom's, receivers needed to be able to make sharp cuts to stop and start quickly. At halftime, the Montreal Players put staples in the bottom of their shoes, and what was a close game in the first half became a blowout in the second as the Montreal players were the only players who could stay on their feet.

In retrospect, I wish I had not gone to that game. For the winners, the Alouettes, it was a home game and the crowd was a home crowd. At the time, there was also great political animosity between Western Canada and French speaking Quebec; it was a bad time to be wearing green and gold in a sea of red and blue. I did not see Tom for a while after that until one day in April of 1978, I looked up and saw he was standing in front of my desk. At that moment, he lifted both hands in the air as though signaling a touchdown and I watched as his pants dropped to the floor.

He had lost 40 pounds. This is what he told me: "I stopped smoking. I got up early, made smoothies, and then I would run for an hour, and hit the gym. I started throwing again and my elbow feels good. I want to make the team if I can. And if I do, I want to be able to make a contribution. I didn't want it to end like last year. So, I have done everything I could possibly think of to do because <u>I never want to look back and wonder what might have been.</u>"

Whoomp, there it is. Pure gold.

I never forgot that, nor will I. In November of 1978, Tom was named most valuable player in the Grey Cup. Edmonton went on to win five consecutive Grey Cups from 1978 to 1982. He never has to look back and wonder what might have been. He played 15 years, went to eight Grey Cups and won five of them. He was a western conference and CFL all-star quarterback in 1974, 1978, and 1979. He won the CFL's Most Outstanding Player Award in 1974.

Including his time with the Rifles, Wilkinson passed for 24,531 yards with 1,754 completions on 2,949 attempts. He threw 172 touchdown passes while being intercepted just 137 times. He also added 1,250 rushing yards and 13 touchdowns.

Tom was always cool and calm. He was at his most dangerous with the game on the line and the clock ticking down. What he lacked in stature and physical gifts he compensated for with intelligence, leadership, unflappable optimism, and commitment.

IF YOU DO SOMETHING OFTEN ENOUGH, YOU WILL GET GOOD AT IT

Like many boys, I had a secret dream of becoming a professional baseball player. It was a secret because it seemed beyond ridiculous, and who could I tell?

I did not know what baseball was when we moved from Bovey, Minnesota to St. Paul after my father's death. I was eight years old and already well behind other kids my age. Throwing and fielding came pretty easy to me, and at one time or another I have played every position on the field, but hitting was always a struggle for me. Although I tried out for my junior high team in the ninth grade, I still couldn't hit.

But, I never stopped working at it, although not necessarily because I thought I would get better. Back then I believed that you were either coordinated or you weren't, and I wasn't. I did it because I enjoyed it. I spent hours bouncing a tennis ball off the outside of the house, pitching shutouts, cutting down runners at second, fielding ground balls like Zoilo Versalles, swinging a level bat like Rich Rollins, and going deep like Harmon Killebrew, all while listening to the Minnesota Twins on the radio.

Every summer night I would go door-to-door to see how many guys I could gather for some kind of baseball game. If there are at least two players, you can hit each other pop flies and grounders. Three allows for batting practice. Five guys on a side allowed for a real game of sorts.

When I was 14, I stumbled upon a book by Dr. Maxwell Maltz titled *Pscho-cybernetics*. Maltz was a plastic surgeon who became fascinated by the reaction of various patients to the results of his surgeries when the bandages came off. He was often baffled. Patients who had major surgeries often responded as though nothing had been done, while other patients who had the most minor of procedures gushed about the amazing difference in their appearance. This tells us something about how we see ourselves, which is to say not very accurately. We know that a negative self-image inhibits one's interactions with others while positive self-images reinforce our interactions.

In this book, I discovered the techniques of "visualization" and "mental practice." Man is a goal-seeking organism. All we need to do is visualize the outcome, plan the steps to the outcome, and then implement the steps. I started to visualize all of the elements of hitting: the sounds of the field, the smell of the grass, "digging in" to the batter's box, setting my stance, the pitcher winding up, the ball being released, my eyes locking on the ball all the way to the bat, and seeing the ball spring off the bat, sailing over second base and landing in no man's land in short center field. I would do it over and over again in my head.

I would practice hitting behind the runner into right field. Right-fielders move toward centerfield for right-handed hitters. This means that there is a lot of room in the right field corner. Hit properly within an inside-out motion, the ball curves around the first baseman and bounces and skips toward the foul line. The right fielder has to come all of the way from right center into foul territory to retrieve the ball. That's triple territory for a right-handed batter and a sure base clearer. The more I visualized, the more consistent I became. The clearer you can see that vision in your mind's eye, the more you can home in on it.

The payoff started to come when I made my first team at the age of 15 at Arlington Playground.

Unlike Phalen Park and Hazel Park, which attracted the best players with their lush infield grass and numerous amenities, Arlington Park was all dirt, hard and unforgiving. If you dove for a ball there, you probably would not get up. It was less than a small city block behind a busy commercial corner along a main bus route into downtown St. Paul with bars and liquor stores predominating the environment. Not the place most parents would allow their children to go to on their own, but it was near where I lived, which was not any better.

We were a terrible team, and I have no memories of any victories or celebratory feelings. That year I played shortstop, centerfield, pitched, and caught. Catching was the worst. The mask would always land face side down in the dirt, and I wonder now why we took them off for pop-ups in the first place. By the end of the game, mud would be running down my face. Foul tip in the groin, collisions at the plate, jammed fingers; you name it, I had it.

Give me a great big patch of grass to defend and I will catch

THE AWFUL TRUTH ABOUT CAREERS IN REAL ESTATE AND WHAT TO DO ABOUT IT

anything I can get to. I have never missed an opportunity to shag flies. I had never worn an actual uniform until then. We went to the basement of the rec-center and rummaged through some old boxes to pull out similar but not matching uniforms. They were from the 30s and smelled of both must and mothballs. They were heavy gray, wool flannel that itched like crazy in the Midwest humidity. If there was a bottom rung in children's sports, this was definitely it. But, it was my uniform and I was No. 1. As silly as it may sound, it was a genuine high point in what had been a largely disappointing life, to that point.

For 45 years, I played either baseball or softball. Never once did I hit a ball out of the park, not even in batting practice. When I was 50, I had one inside the park home run. I am 5 feet 7 inches and 125 pounds, so I am not built to go deep; what I have is warning track power. If I tried to hit home runs, I would only fly out.

But, there is a no man's land between the infield and outfield that cannot be defended. I saw the field as a tennis court where all I had to do was clear the net, or in this case the infield, and drop it right in front of the outfield. I lead off. It is my job to get on base to, as we say, set the table for the big guys. I worked on every aspect of my game from base running to ground balls, from fly balls to throwing for greater accuracy.

Malcolm Gladwell in his book *Outliers* notes that 10,000 hours of practice is what it takes to achieve mastery or what I would call "personal best." I just kept on playing, practicing, and trying to improve. As I did more playing, opportunities opened up and I was being invited to better teams. The years went by, teammates retired and new one's joined. I met a lot of people; people who have friends and family, who know my work ethic and what I stand for.

In 1999, I was recruited from the Fountain Valley Barons to Top Gun San Diego, a highly competitive over-50 Senior Men's tournament team. During this time, there were a number of changes on the team, including new management, sponsorship, and numerous player changes, but early in 2001, the team started to gel.

I worked out with a personal trainer and played on three local teams weekly. We started winning tournaments and getting a reputation. I was in great shape, fielding and throwing well, and my hitting was getting better almost weekly.

But, my lower back and left hip were starting to bother me. As a right-handed hitter and thrower, I was always turning my body hard left. Base running is all left turns so that was putting even more strain on it. I was still performing well, but I was paying the price. I had it checked out and was told it was a piriformis injury. The doctors gave me some stretches to do and I started taking Vioxx.

My back was not getting better, but it had not started to affect my game yet. Our tournament season was to conclude with the Senior Softball World Championships in mid-September and I planned to take some time off after that.

The Western Nationals were held in Roseville, California, the last weekend in August. I was hurting, but still playing at the top of my game with the help of Vioxx and the hotel hot tub. We won that tournament and were on our way to the World Championship in Las Vegas to take on the Eastern National Champions.

Then came Sept. 11, 2001. The airlines were grounded with the tournament scheduled to start on the 14. It's only about a five-hour drive for me, so I didn't plan to fly. How the team from Hawaii got there, I will never know.

There was so much uncertainty and no guarantee that there would even be a tournament. It was not a very difficult decision for me. I had worked hard for this, and when in doubt, always do what is on the schedule.

Since this was my "World Series," I decided to go first class and had made a reservation at the Four Seasons. It was a good choice. Vegas was in the process of disgorging terrified visitors who stood in front of the hotels looking for others to split the cost of a charter flight. Remember, at this point, no one had any idea what was going to happen next, and the last place most wanted to be was in Las Vegas.

The Four Seasons sits on top of the Mandalay Bay Hotel, and I had a great view of the airport. The only other guest on my floor was rumored by the staff to be a Saudi prince. I was curious about this since there was a man with an automatic rifle standing by the elevator. I am pretty sure they had vetted me because, despite my best efforts to engage him, he would not acknowledge my presence. As for me, well, I have never felt safer.

Vegas cleared out over the next couple of days, but most of the team found ways to get there. Best time ever to be in Vegas. When the tournament concluded, we were the National Champions, I played great despite what later was diagnosed as radiculopathy with acute neurological deficit, and I was named to the All World Team.

I know what you're thinking, "Is that it? Are you kidding me, or what? You played softball with some old men?"

Remember, it all depends on how you look at things. I know it is not the World Series and it is not the pros. What did I get? I got to play in a few thousand softball games and practices. I got to run, hit, catch, and throw things. I stayed in good shape, and I have extraordinarily good health to this day. Not to be overlooked, this involvement with like-minded people was a target rich environment for potential referrals. So, in a way, I got paid to do what I love to do. When I was going full speed trying to rundown a fly ball, I never thought about what team I was on or where we were playing.

Sometimes things take longer than we think they should. Maybe we just have to put in those 10,000 hours, and if that takes a lifetime, what does it matter? I always wanted to play against the best competition I could find. The victories and the championships are just as sweet as if I had been paid for them.

KEEPING THE FAITH

Ya gotta believe! You may experience occasional self-doubt in the face of setbacks or criticism. That is normal. It is a success mechanism that reminds us to take nothing for granted, and to be mindful of our thoughts and actions.

It is faith that propels us to get back up when we have been knocked down. Not to be confused with religion, faith is the understanding that as long as we are using our abilities to create positive change, everything will unfold in due time.

There is no downside to building a better you. What would happen if you were healthier? What would happen if you were a more aware and appreciative partner? What would happen if you attracted more like-minded people to you?

The most attractive aspect of building a real estate business is that it provides an extraordinary platform from which to give value to your community while doing the activities you were meant to do.

So the bottom line is this: it is difficult to build a rewarding business because of the law of supply and demand. There is an extreme abundance of look alike, fungible real estate agents and a very limited number of transactions. The vast majority of this oversupply is all competing for a very small percentage of those transactions, those ripe buyers and sellers who do not already know someone in real estate. What are the odds of that?

Your choices are to become a prospector and a salesperson, generate leads and close deals, or discount your services. Or, you can achieve mastery in the art of community building and real estate services through constant and ongoing self-improvement.

Building your own community of like-minded people allows you to eliminate all other competition and solve the problem of too many agents and not enough closings. Each and every day, be better in every way.

CHAPTER 18

THE POSSIBILITIES ARE ENDLESS

"Sometimes the slightest things change the directions of our lives, the merest breath of a circumstance, a random moment that connects like a meteorite striking the Earth. Lives have swiveled and changed direction on the strength of a chance remark."
—BRYCE COURTENAY

Most of those who pass through real estate never build anything of value during their brief struggle. They cannot see the bigger picture because they are always focused on finding a deal and closing it. They work too hard for too little. But, the real estate business can be fun if you purposefully meet people in the process of doing things you enjoy.

If you adopt and adhere to the principals in this book, you will build a personal services business based on referrals. This is your ultimate goal; your role is trusted adviser. You get there by building a better you, one certain, well-planned step at a time by actively engaging in consumer education regarding real estate.

But, life and change are inseparable. Your personal journey could take you to places you never imagined and provide you with opportunities you never anticipated. People in the real estate business often wind up in politics. Tomorrow you could be launching a gluten-free line of baked goods or becoming a personal trainer.

One of my former associates now operates Bliss Yoga, relying on the same principles she followed as an extraordinarily successful real estate practitioner within the same community. She was a referral magnate. Before real estate she was a teacher. Teach and you will learn.

It is you, it is not what you do. The foundation of your businesses is the community you build that can take you anywhere. So, while you may have begun this leg of your journey thinking, "What the heck, I bet I could sell some houses," you will discover that it is not even about that.

It is about people. More specifically, it is about the people you select to add to your community and how effectively you interact with them. Everything else is just temporary.

REINVENTION IS THE SPICE OF LIFE

It had taken 14 years but by 2006, I had built from scratch a full-service real estate and mortgage brokerage. I had a 4,500 square-foot, ocean-view office in Carlsbad, California, three well-paid employees, 40 licensees doing real estate and making loans, but I also had a business overhead of nearly $45,000 per month. That is stress.

On the plus side, I also had the fruits of those labors close at hand. I had over 800 new and adaptive reuse lofts in various parts of Southern California expected to close escrow over an 18-month period to bring in around $600 each.

Unfortunately, that ship sunk in the harbor before ever tying up. The bubble burst. Those lofts mostly went back to the banks, and by the end of the year I had locked the doors for good. We ran out of borrowers and the pendulum swung the other way. The end of a long chapter of my life had arrived, but unknown to me at the time was that a strange new chapter was about to unfold.

"Annyeong-haseyo?"

"Annyeong-haseyo" is a Korean greeting that means about the same as, "Hi, how ya' doin?"

In July of 2007, I packed some things, shut up the house and drove to Los Angeles to assume my duties at 3800 Wilshire Boulevard as Sales Manager of the Mercury lofts, an ill-fated adaptive reuse of the old Getty Oil building. This building was located on the corner of Wilshire Boulevard and Western Avenue, directly across the street from the legendary live music venue and art deco masterpiece, The Wiltern Theatre. Welcome to Koreatown.

MERCURY RISING: A CASE STUDY IN MARKET ANALYSIS

The Mercury is a tale of bad business, bad design, bad decisions, poor execution, and the damage done by unbridled hubris. I would spend the next two years in that environment being challenged in ways I could never have imagined, but I had reached a point where I had so much experience that you could pretty much toss me the keys to any business and I would figure it out.

My job was to develop an onsite sales team to persuade Koreans to buy lofts they did not like in a building they were superstitious of in a crime ridden section of Los Angeles for substantially more than they were worth. How bad could that be? By 10:05 on my first morning, the iPod we used to play music in the sales center had been stolen from the sales office. Eventually the plasma TV on which we would show virtual tours disappeared, and unknown to me at the time, things were about to get a lot more interesting.

THE AWFUL TRUTH ABOUT CAREERS IN REAL ESTATE AND WHAT TO DO ABOUT IT

Defining the challenges

The developer was a very large company with lots of large and complicated projects in their background, but the project manager had come from city government and had never done anything remotely akin to real estate development. She knew she was in over her head, and there are two ways to handle that. One is to turn to and trust in seasoned veterans who have been doing their jobs for decades and to seek out their advice and counsel as part of a more deliberative decision making process. The other path is to choose isolation, avoid contact with the front-lines, be unresponsive to the point of dereliction, and whenever questioned or challenged, become aggressive and condescending.

The developer shunned the building and avoided any meaningful discussions about actually closing the lofts. Meetings, to the extent we had any, were by phone or held in the developer's offices rather than on site.

If it were my first project, I would have wanted to be there every day. You know, just to get a feel for how it is done and maybe learn something. When I or others made suggestions she did not agree with, she did not say we were wrong and then back it up. Instead her stock response was a sarcastic, "Maybe I should go over to USC and see if I can get back the money I paid for my MBA?"

Not to put too fine a point on it, but I am pretty sure she signed something when she enrolled at USC that says they are not responsible for whether or not she knows anything when she leaves there. But, if it would have helped her out, I could honestly vouch for her premise.

When you analyze the situation, the single biggest obstacle to the success of the project was the seller, in this case the project manager, and so if you judge people by the results they get, she would definitely deserve to get her money back. Too bad California teachers, who invested their pensions, cannot get their money back. She spent $100 million to transform a building that eventually sold in bulk for $27 million. Along the way, she snubbed her nose at a $61 million offer for the same remaining units.

Learning the hard way

In May of 2006, an off-site sales office was opened with interest so high that there was a line around the block. Two weeks later sales began.

This event turned into a free-for-all since Koreans tend to resist queuing-up. They are also very technologically advanced, have the latest smartphones, and a large network of friends and family. Unknown to the sales team was that as each buyer reserved a condo, they would send photos, floor plans, and the price they paid to everyone out on the street.

With sales so robust, the developer decided to start bumping prices on the most popular floor plans as each new wave of potential buyers came through the door. You can imagine how well that went over. "But Mr. Kim paid only five-fifty!" With plenty of bad feelings spreading through Koreatown, sales peaked with 84 of the 220 lofts being reserved. Most of these never closed escrow.

Hardhat tours began in early 2007, and when the buyers saw the finished product, the kimchi really hit the fan. Most cancelled.

The sales team in place at the time lacked the experience to negotiate with Koreans and so, in order to save some sales, they began to induce sales with promises of more or better parking and free storage in addition to those already legally assigned to the loft. See the problem?

After the first wave of buyers moved in, sales dried up and so did the low-down stated income loans that had funded the first wave of sales. The project would need to close 70 units in order to be approved for Fannie Mae financing.

Having scorched Koreatown, the seller concluded that local Koreans were not their market after all and hired a firm by the name of Interconnect to schlepp the marketing materials, all in English by the way, around Asia and the Middle East. Interconnect was never heard from again.

Due to anticipated demand, the developer made a fateful error that would take substantial time and effort to overcome — they decided to exclude resale brokers from participating. Not cooperating with resale brokers is one of the dumbest things a developer can do since it costs nothing unless a closing occurs, and it stirs up a lot of traffic. In Koreatown, everyone is interconnected, and the brokers simply bad-mouthed the building far and wide, in particular, the rumors about it being haunted.

In the case of The Mercury, thousands of dollars were spent each week on advertising that did nothing. But then, like all of the sales materials, these ads were in English. By ignoring Korean culture, the developer did not realize that almost all communication would need to be in Korean and that Koreans all have brokers; they would not make a move without them. The client ultimately receives some of the money paid to their broker, and while this might be unlawful, it is part of the culture.

The developers had painted themselves into a corner. There were no buyers to be found in Asia or the Middle East. The perceived market for whom the lofts were supposedly designed, "hip, young, generation 2.0 Koreans" were too young to have a down payment and too hip to live there unless their parents bought it for them. In reality, no such stereotype exists. I never met any while I was there. They may dress trendy, but they do what their parents and grandparents tell them to do.

The building had been abandoned for decades, which is never good for a building. But in this case, it gave rise to a great sense of foreboding among Koreans who had come to believe the building was haunted. This sense of foreboding was only deepened by the two suicides that dove from the roof deck on the 23rd floor onto Wilshire Boulevard during my tenure.

Now that the building had been rehabilitated, it led two lives. During the day, it was very quiet since it was almost vacant except for a few shops adjacent to the lobby. But in the evening the lobby would fill with beautiful young Korean women and a few boys dressed in the latest party fashion.

At first, it wasn't clear what was happening. Then a tenant on the 15th floor vanished and dozens of boxes of Korean passports, driver's licenses, and other identification were discovered. These young people were victims of human trafficking and would be picked up in the lobby and taken to underground clubs by wealthy Korean businessmen. So the building also had that going for it.

NOTHING IS PERFECT

Whether it is a single listing or 220 at the same address, it is important to determine the conditions, positive or negative, that impact the sale and subsequently the marketing and ultimate closing.

Some of my first listings were distressed properties; this resulted from a relationship I had with an asset manager at a Savings and Loan. When a borrower would get behind, the S and L would call me and give me the name and address of the delinquent borrower so that I would stop by to make contact with the borrower and get the details. Unfortunately, the nature of these properties is that they usually represent the least desirable properties in the diciest areas. But what the hell, I was young, ambitious, and armed.

All of the really good real estate was gone a hundred years ago and most of the rest of us settle for what we can afford. Nothing is perfect so whenever I analyze a piece of real estate, I seek to answer certain questions, such as what are the strengths and what are the challenges? Who is the potential buyer and what does she want? How do we reach her?

Koreans, for the most part, prefer new and modern and have an advanced sense of style. They do not really like old buildings and the bones of the Mercury were from 1960.

The building had been gutted and rehabilitated. The original design was for 10 lofts per floor, but real estate was hot during the planning stages and so they decided to cram in 12. The result was a number of odd floorplans that did not appeal to the Korean buyer. The door to the I Plan opened right into a wall so you would have to turn sideways to go through the door. Feng Shui? No way!

Adding two more lofts per floor required renumbering the lofts resulting in numerous title problems, but the biggest problem was the impact on parking. The garage was designed in the early 60s for office workers and was intended to accommodate two American cars between the pillars. Now they would need to jam in three. SUVs would not fit into many of the tiny spaces. Many of the spots were on the roof and open to the elements and were highly undesireable.

The Mercury had only two floor plans that had enclosed bedrooms. An almost insurmountable problem for most Koreans seeing as these were intended to be family gathering places. If there were a Richter scale for seriously bad ideas with one being a minor gaffe, the seller pushed all the way to 11 on the

THE POSSIBILITIES ARE ENDLESS

Spinal Tap amp.

Almost everything that could have been done wrong had been. The kitchen cabinets, which the developer insisted were "luxurious," were in fact extremely low quality, painted pressed-board more suitable for a garage than an upscale loft.

Michelle Lee brought her mother by to see the loft she had purchased from me and before we got out of the model, her mother walked over to one of the cabinet doors, opened it part way and then turned to me and asked why they were so cheaply made.

I smiled and said, "So that you won't feel badly when you rip them down and replace them with something you like."

There is no point pretending that a thing is something that it is not or that low quality is luxury when it is obviously not. Be realistic about your situation because you must find a buyer for every property regardless of the circumstances.

PROJECT ANALYSIS

On the one hand we have an old office building believed by the most likely buyers to be haunted, that had been converted to tiny open spaces with bad floor plans and cheap finishes being offered to people who do not want them for prices unlikely to appraise.

Financing was nearly impossible to get since the Mercury was a long way from obtaining Fannie Mae approval, and liar's loans had been pulled from the market. If that wasn't bad enough, on the opposite corner was a construction project to be known as Solair Wilshire, a brand new state-of-the-art luxury high rise with the types of floor plans and finishes that Koreans desire, and unlimited parking for about the same price per square foot. Even worse, they were paying full broker co-op fees.

The Mercury was overpriced. The pro-forma was overly optimistic as price appreciation was projected based on recent historical gains, but the market peaked just as sales began.

Strengths

"You've got to accentuate the positive and eliminate the negative."
—JONNY MERCER

Location, Live/Work Zoning, History, Money Flow, Architect: Those five things need to be emphasized in order to create value sufficient in the mind of the buyer to justify above market prices, or at least you have to try.

- **Location**

It did have location… if you were Korean.

I am a country boy. I live up a hill off of a narrow winding road. I do not like big cities, and the Mercury was smack dab in the middle of the things I do not like the most: noise, stink, grime, and an atmosphere of random mayhem and extreme chaos.

But, the building was not going anywhere. Still, it was in a good location with its proximity to Hollywood and Downtown Los Angeles. But, its main feature as a location was its presence in K-Town. Additionally, Koreans are often fully adapted to high-rise living since it is the standard in many Korean cities.

Thus, it was important to learn everything I could about Koreatown, as well as the building. For two days before I went on site, I walked the streets of Koreatown, poked around in the shops and tried to get the vibe of the place. It wasn't all good but it was vibrant.

- **Live/Work Zoning**

THE POSSIBILITIES ARE ENDLESS

As a business owner, it had always been my intention to stop renting office space and buy a location. Since the Mercury was a converted office building, it qualified for live/work zoning. That aspect of the building had not been properly promoted, and most potential buyers were unaware of that feature. Here again, the local brokers and agents would have been a tremendous asset had they been consulted.

· History

I studied the history of Koreatown and learned that The Immigration and Nationality Act of 1965 relaxed immigration rules resulting in large numbers of South Koreans immigrating to Los Angeles where they settled in the neighborhoods around Western Avenue and Wilshire Avenue. Here they found inexpensive housing and a plethora of small retail shops on heavily traveled streets that were perfect for mom and pop businesses.

They came throughout the 70s and 80s bringing their culture, their cuisine, and their attitude. They clustered together in an area of less than three square miles with more than 120,000 residents. Two-thirds of the residents of this community were born outside of the United States.

As I walked the streets of Koreatown, it was impossible to ignore how much this felt like being in another country. "Second Seoul" the residents call it. All advertising and most signs are in Korean. But, in many ways this was a new Koreatown. It is an up from the ashes Phoenix-like rebirth that sprang from the fires of the Los Angeles riots.

"Sa-I-Gu"

It was April 29, 1992. The Koreans call it Sa-I-Gu — four-twenty-nine. Miles from Koreatown, in Simi Valley, California, an all-white jury acquitted four white police officers in the videotaped beating of African American, Rodney King. By May 4, when the smoke cleared, literally, 53 people would be dead, 35 by gunshot.

In six days of rioting, over a billion dollars in damage was done, 4,000 people were injured, 12,000 were arrested, 3,500 fires were started, and 1,100 buildings were destroyed.

Korean and Asian businesses were targeted. Roughly 90 percent of Korean family-owned businesses were burned, forcing them to leave the area to find new locations. This would turn out to be a nugget of information beyond the obvious. While only one Korean was killed as a result of Sa-I-Gu, his tragic and senseless death left the Korean community with no one to blame. Edward Song Lee was responding to a call for help from a Korean-owned business, and while rushing to the scene, was shot and killed by other Koreans who mistook him for a looter.

More than 20 years later, there is little evidence of Sa-I-Gu or of the Koreatown that existed prior to Sa-I-Gu. From dilapidated storefronts and squalid housing, the area has literally been rebuilt, one building at a time, creating a strange hodgepodge of vastly different architectural styles and scale.

To a long-time resident of Koreatown, there is no forgetting and there is a two-way racism smoldering beneath the surface. Before Sa-I-Gu, the Korean shops were patronized by mostly African Americans. There was a simmering tension between the two groups, which was not diminished any by the televised images of African Americans looting and burning Korean stores.

What the seller did not understand was that those "generation 2.0" Koreans for which the lofts were designed were no different than their parents. Sa-I-Gu was the catalyst for a reinvigorated ethnic awareness and pride. Second generation Korean-Americans, having been born and reared here, tried initially to distance themselves from their parents who did not speak the language or understand American culture. Sa-I-Gu changed all of that. Second generation Korean-Americans began to appreciate how difficult it had been for their parents, many of whom never completely recovered. They saw what happened to their parent's stores and businesses and that no one came to help them but family and friends — other Koreans.

Most second generation Korean Americans now embrace their Koreanness and the importance of their family and heritage. When it comes to an important decision, such as buying real estate, several generations might be involved in the process. Second generation Koreans are frequently seen in the company of their parents and grandparents, whom they revere. It is part of the culture to want to please one's elders and not disappoint them.

Unfortunately, the seller failed to take an in-depth look at the actual marketplace. They cared nothing for the culture or the circumstances that would ultimately drive buyer decision-making. The changing attitudes in Koreatown after Sa-I-Gu carried over to the business of the Mercury since the buyers were 95 percent Korean, and the project manager was an African American woman who, unfortunately wore her disdain for Koreans on her sleeve. There was so much bad blood between her and the owner of the retail space that he eventually wound up suing the developer.

- **Money Flow**

Another significant strength was that Koreatown was awash in money that was rapidly losing its buying power. Money was pouring in from Asia and was showing up on the streets of K-Town in the form of Bentleys, Maybachs, Breitlings, and Gucci's, as well as the reopening of dozens of long abandoned businesses, boutiques, bars, and restaurants.

I also learned that in order to lower the value of its currency, the government of South Korea had been progressively relaxing foreign investment limits. In 2006, it was raised from $300,000 to $1 million. Then in 2007, it was increased to $3 million. Since the effect of this action was to gradually lower the purchasing power of the won, there was actually an urgency to invest or spend it.

By the time I arrived at the Mercury, the first wave of buyers had closed escrow and moved in. Since there were only a dozen or so of these, I went through the files to determine what I could about their profile. Some had other residences in Southern California, others had addresses in South Korea, and both groups were obviously investors.

As it turned out, many of the buyers of lofts and condos in Koreatown were people who left Koreatown to reopen their businesses in other communities from Fullerton to Tehachapi to Mira Loma immediately following Sa-I-Gu. They wanted to return on weekends for the food and the nightlife and to reconnect with old friends who remained in the area.

· **The Architect**

Not everything has a history, but when it does, it can be a selling feature. Most people see an old high-rise and perceive it like a tree or a rock, as though it had just always been there. The old Getty building had a pretty rough life. She began life as the toast of the town, the first building in Los Angeles to rise above 13 stories and the last to be designed by legendary architect Claud Beelman under the exacting supervision of J. Paul Getty himself, to be the World Head Quarters for Getty Oil in 1963. By telling the story of the architect, I was able to focus on the historical significance in terms of Los Angeles. That way I could, to a certain extent, overcome their antipathy regarding the age of the building.

THE POSSIBILITIES ARE ENDLESS

For 40 years, Claud Beelman was the most prolific and imaginative architect of his time. Ten of his creations have already been added to The National Register of Historic Places, and many others have received some sort of noteworthy designation from their local community. The very history of Los Angeles' most dynamic decades can be traced through his more than two dozen remaining works.

Very few architects receive widespread recognition among lay people. We tend to take their work for granted, living in and among their creations without ever wondering how, from once raw dirt, sprang this thing of form and function. We march right past stately old buildings and soaring skyscrapers as though they were rocks or trees, eyes focused on the sidewalk ahead, while unnoticed by us, the spirit of the past is alive in their work.

Architects are hybrids; part artist, part engineer, all dreamer. They see things that are not there and set about to make them out of lumber, steel, concrete, stone, glass, and sweat. When it comes to American mid-century architects, Frank Lloyd Wright has gotten most of the attention. Wright's work is also widely recognized due to its distinctly mid-century look, horizontal lines, and integration into its surroundings.

Though Wright's reputation left little room for other architects to become well known, he had many outstanding contemporaries including, Stiles O. Clements who designed The Wiltern, Irving Gill, Henry Eames, Buckminster Fuller, Mies van der Rohe and the recently rediscovered Claud Beelman.

Changing Functions Drive Changing Form

Beelman had an ever-evolving style that tended to mirror the dominant themes of early and mid-20th century. He did not follow design trends; he invented them. The work of his life evolved through separate and distinct architectural genres, and it is apparent in the diversity of his creations.

From Beaux Arts, to Art Deco, to Streamline Moderne, his works reflect the history and dynamics of a nation evolving from an agrarian economy, to a manufacturing economy, to a business information economy. His early works represent the optimism of a nation on the verge of major advances in science, engineering, technology, commerce, and prosperity.

In the 20s he built hotel apartments for a nation moving into cities. He built the meeting place at which Los Angeles power brokers met to divvy up the opportunities. He built office buildings for a nation's growing business needs. He built banks, a post office, a department store, and renovated a theatre. He designed a museum, and in the infancy of television, he designed the first building specifically created for the new medium. Born before the automobile, he embraced the dynamics of change and reflected it through his work. In 1924, he designed one of the first parking garages.

Little is known about Beelman prior to his arrival in Los Angeles. He was born in Ohio in 1883. The 1910 Census shows him as a draftsman. It seems doubtful that he would have had much formal training. He arrived with a wife and daughter sometime around 1920, and by 1923, had completed the Culver Hotel.

The 1920s were a busy decade for Beelman. From 1923 through 1929, his firm Curlett and Beelman erected, among many others, three examples of Renaissance Revival: the Culver Hotel, Cooper Arms, and the Barker Brothers Building, now the Mayfair Hotel.

When Art Deco emerged, Beelman led the way with the Art Deco Garfield, the building at Ninth and Broadway, the building at 816 South Grand, and The Roosevelt.

THE POSSIBILITIES ARE ENDLESS

Perhaps his most interesting work of this period was created as a place for the movers and shakers of the time, the L.A. Elks Club No. 99, which opened in 1925. Inspired by the discovery of King Tut's Tomb, Beelman created a landmark neo-gothic overlooking MacArthur Park. Both eerily strange and boldly magnificent, the Egyptian Revival masterpiece is a collection of exterior art ranging from angels erupting from plinths to a row of soldiers' faces surrounding the building. Though not currently being used as a hotel, it remains a popular location for filming due to its amazing lobby.

As this decade was drawing to a close, Beelman was putting the finishing touches on what was to become his most notable work, the truly splendid and extraordinarily detailed Art Deco masterpiece, the Eastern Columbia building. Both opulent and optimistic, the Eastern Columbia marked the end of the Age of Innocence. The crash of 1929 was a stark reminder of the evils of excess and a new cautious austerity permeated the American psyche.

The America of the '30s was a serious place. We were recovering from our first brush with harsh and brutal reality. If you had a job, probably in a factory, you were happy to have it. The focus now was less on show and more on greater efficiency, and that meant speed. Form was entirely subordinate to function.

The pace of life began to accelerate and so did our fascination with speed and the future. Design themes reflected the need for speed and shapes became aerodynamic. Even stationary items appeared to be moving as they reflected sleek, flowing, and rounded images. Note the similarities between an Airstream Trailer and Buck Roger's spaceship.

Americans did not want to think about the recent past so they looked forward. In 1937, Beelman completed what is today the Millard Sheets Center for The Arts at Fairplex. The 12,000 square foot structure was originally designed as The Los

THE AWFUL TRUTH ABOUT CAREERS IN REAL ESTATE AND WHAT TO DO ABOUT IT

Angeles County Fair Gallery and paid for by the Public Works Administration, which was formed to create post-depression jobs.

The industrial age peaked after World War II, and a new era of corporate information processing began. The need for office space drove the final phase of Beelman's career.

His last few buildings remind us of the era of the corporation: sleek, efficient, and all business. During this period, he designed a bank annex with virtually no architectural detailing except that its reflective skin mirrors the activity on the street. In 1955, he completed the Superior Oil Building, now The Standard Hotel. The lobby of The Standard today is an eclectic mix of business icons.

So who cares, right? What does it mean to someone growing a business?

We solve problems. If there were no problems, people would buy and sell real estate online. The Mercury had a lot of problems, but every piece of real estate has utility, and that utility has value to someone.

The architect in this case is a marketable strength. A high-rise loft is just a chunk of air in the sky, but if you want someone to buy one for a half a million bucks, you need to build value in the mind of the potential buyer. If you are going to sell an ugly chunk of air for too much money, you had better have a pretty good story to tell.

Everything that Claude Beelman learned in 20 years of architecture reached its crescendo at the corner of Wilshire and Western when in 1963, the 22-story Getty Building was opened.

In this case, there was romance and history surrounding that chunk of air, but when I arrived onsite no one knew who Claud

THE POSSIBILITIES ARE ENDLESS

Beelman was. Who cared? If it was real estate and it was for sale, you could not talk people out of buying it. But this time things really were different.

STRATEGY

To me, the answer was obvious. Since money was flowing out of Korea and Asia to the West, there were ample buyers still in Korea, but they would not be looking for a specific property, they would be looking for boots on the ground in Koreatown to locate the best deals. They would be calling brokers in Koreatown on their smartphones. Korean brokers in the suburbs around LA could bring us the buyers who were looking for a return to Koreatown.

The brokers were angry that the seller did not turn to them in the first place. I made a strong argument for increasing the broker co-op fee to the customary three percent they would receive for selling virtually anything else.

Advertising

Advertising to the consumer had not resulted in producing **any** qualified prospects. On the other hand, the brokers had been very successful advertising in their own "down and dirty" style and Korean messaging. Instead of hiring a top Korean ad agency, I recommended using co-op advertising dollars as a sales incentive for the brokers. We still had some control over the message and we split the cost after the ad ran.

Signage

Our sign traffic consisted largely of people who had stopped to get coffee or juice in the retail area and were often looking for a bathroom. Most thought we were leasing.

Flex walls

We needed to demonstrate how the large, open rooms could be enclosed so I arranged for some flex walls to be installed in several of the open floor plans.

Reaching out to the brokers and agents

Now that brokers and agents could earn a typical fee, I still had to overcome their resentment toward the developer. But, that was only part of the problem. The brokers and agents did not know enough to be anything more than an obstacle. They saw their role as getting their buyer the very best deal. The result was a succession of low-ball offers. Having been a franchise owner and an independent broker, I knew that the key to agent success is education, and so I turned to my old standby, broker education. My message was "help me help you make money at the Mercury." The question I am most often asked about my experience is whether or not I speak Korean. I do not... but I do speak broker.

Seller financing

Rather than lower the prices to market value, the seller came up with a seller assisted financing incentive dubbed the "soft second." The soft second was probably illegal; it was so complicated that it was hard to know for sure. But, it did not matter since, despite schlepping my broker-training program to offices all-over LA and Orange County, as well as making 40 sales, none of these would ever close.

From November of 2007 to April of 2008, the seller prolonged the closings without any explanation to the buyers, many of whom became extremely upset about the delay. Some were forced into temporary homelessness as a result. Finally, in April, word came that the seller was ready to close the first six soft seconds, and at the end of a lengthy conference call, all of

THE POSSIBILITIES ARE ENDLESS

the associated documents were packaged and sent via courier to the developer's home office in Cleveland for signature. And then?

Nothing. The whereabouts of those files remains a mystery, but the result was that the seller was unable to fund the "soft seconds." No reason was ever provided to the buyers. Buyers and brokers became increasingly upset about delays and lack of communication from the developer. Many had been left homeless, living in hotels and waiting to close escrow. At the same time, Solair Wilshire, the new condo project across the street began selling.

"Plan B" the builder's "spec lock"

After the disappearance of the soft second files, it was determined that a new program would be introduced in the form of an interest rate buy-down. After weeks of planning, it was further determined that I would call in all of the buyers and their brokers, take away the soft seconds, and spin them into the interest rate buy-down.

It was a Saturday morning. I would be starting the morning with my two most productive brokers, Brandon Park and Sam Oh. They had introduced multiple buyers to the building, had both been waiting nearly a year for substantial commissions, and were very eager to hear the new plan.

I do not remember much of what was said, but I could feel the anger swelling in the room and I do recall "bait and switch," and the threats of lawsuits. I asked them to give me a few moments.

I could feel myself starting to lose it. They were right, and I had been pushing this rock up the same hill since I got there. You just want to do your job and move on. It was fight or flight. I shut down my computer and put it in my bag. I cleaned a few things out of my desk and was about to head for my car. But, that isn't how I'm wired. I was weary and disappointed. Then I thought, "What the hell, it would be way more fun to get fired."

With the possibility of losing the buyers and a resulting lawsuit against the developer, I elected to try to "find the Market" and set about to renegotiate as many soft second buyers as could be salvaged. This led to significant momentum that carried us through September.

From Saturday morning until Monday night, I negotiated 31 new sales from these buyers at prices that were reflective of the market. On Tuesday, we shipped the box to the developer with a letter that said, "Take it or leave it."

They took them. This was the market and these contracts were clearly a reflection of the market. Then came "Black October." The global economic meltdown did not spare Asia. Some of the potential buyers in our pipeline lost significant amounts of money and others were frightened into withdrawing and waiting. But by November, the shock seemed to have given way to resolve and interest was picking up.

Bulk sale

The developer was ready to throw in the towel, and let it be known that an offer for all remaining units would be considered. Working with two Korean brokers, Young Lee and Gene Kim, we obtained an offer from an investor for $61,000,000. The developer continually delayed responding, and declared a moratorium on sales from November of 2008 until April of 2009, when the developer revealed that it had accepted an offer of $27,000,000.

So it was over. Not with a bang, but with a whimper.

THE POSSIBILITIES ARE ENDLESS

In many of life's detours, there is often a back story, and if you are lucky, sometimes more than one. These stories remind us that we are just passing through a place in time. We are part of a cycle of many dimensions: birth, growth, decline, disease, renewal, obsolescence, and senescence. Those cycles are entwined in the lives of others, and if we step back, we can see a rich tapestry being woven; not always what we want, but the possibilities are endless.

CONCLUSION

One must be something of an optimist to set out to write a book. It is a long and unpredictable voyage, unless you are Stephen King... and I am no Stephen King, despite the horror story that is the truth about the real estate business.

Nor did I just wake up one morning and decide that I wanted to write a book. This journey began over 25 years ago with my first attempt, "101 Things You Should Know About Careers in Real Estate," and I'm just now finishing. I know more than I did then, but it is evident to me in looking back that I was building on certain ideas that were not always in harmony with how the industry operates. I've seen a lot of people come and go, so I know what the causes of failure are.

I've seen what works, and I marvel at how few practitioners do those things... consistently. As an advocate of continual self-improvement, my training programs are ongoing, so I have done substantial research, written hundreds of articles, and designed numerous training programs starting in 1980 when I began managing my first office.

The opportunity to finish that book came at the height of the real estate boom when I was contacted by The American Management Association to author a book about real estate careers. I had worked for weeks trying to master their submission process, and then came the crash and they closed their real estate division. I remarked that they picked a hell of a time to drop real estate books just when things were getting interesting. But it would have been a very different book; it would have been one of those boring, stodgy, passive business books that sound like a committee wrote them.

CONCLUSION

I wanted the reader to benefit from the real-life experiences that derive from almost 40 years in the field, doing almost everything that can be done. I wanted to broaden my perspective and to deepen my understanding of real estate, the business, and people. My book is based on first-hand experience, and the system I have created works for those who are faithful to it.

As in writing a book, you need to be an optimist to build a real estate business. Day one is a blank sheet of paper; you start with nothing. You write a book the same way you build a real estate business — show up on time and do the important things first.

The writer needs to turn ideas into words, one word at a time. A personal services business such as real estate is built one person at a time.

You also need patience to write a book and to build a referral business. No matter what you do, it will take some time. You want to jump right to the end before the work is done. Focus on meeting people and asking for listing referrals. Present a CMA to any property owner who will listen. These are your words, sentences, paragraphs, and chapters.

A writer needs to have confidence in his subject matter and the courage to face criticism and disappointment. I have confidence because I possess the combination of knowledge and experience that leads to understanding. A writer has to have faith — faith that his work will get published and that his book will be purchased, faith that his words will be read and, hopefully, all the way to the end.

I finished that line in early 2016, anticipating that the book was on schedule to be published in late spring or early summer. Now it is May of 2017. What happened? Another obstacle.

I had contracted with Atlantic Publishing of Ocala, Florida to co-publish the book. They charge a flat fee of $3,995.00 and promise, "There are no hidden extras or fees."

The process they describe for publishing a book started out slowly…then petered out. Nothing ever happened.

Then on September 13, 2016, a full eleven months after entering into the contract, I received this email from the publisher of Atlantic Publishing Group, Doug Brown.

> *"Hi George – I know we have disappointed you thus far, and I would really like to get this book project turned around, and turned around fast.*
>
> *We have failed you miserably in the communicating with you and keeping this book on a reasonable production time line.*
>
> *At this point I have read over all the notes from Colleen & Rebekah. I have read over your email letter to Rebekah. I have spoken to Jackie, Meg, Colleen, Crystal and Rebekah either in person or by phone about your book and concerns. I take the matter very seriously and my goal is to rectify the situation.*
>
> *I would like to set up a time at your convenience to get the book back on track, and published, to your satisfaction. Please let me know what is convenient – I'm also available in the evening or weekends to discuss, and get the book back on track.*
>
> *Sincerely – Doug"*

So, we had that conversation. And since I had already paid $2,397, I had no reason to doubt that the things promised would happen and happen quickly.

CONCLUSION

Nothing happened until early October when I received an invoice from Atlantic Publishing Group for $1,885.47 for editing. The so-called editing involved not a single consultation and was done by an intern.

When I objected to this additional and undisclosed charge, I received an unsigned letter from Atlantic Publishing Group dated November 8, 2016, "Atlantic Publishing Group, Inc. is terminating said contract."

As a matter of law, this was a bilateral not a unilateral contract and so legally Atlantic Publishing Group is in breach of that agreement.

But as a practical matter, I had wasted over a year and had little to show for it.

We live in an era where corporations do whatever they want without fear of legal consequences. As a result, contracts rarely afford much benefit to consumers and if I wanted to sue for specific performance I'd have to go to Florida to do it.

As with so many things in life, success doesn't always come with the first attempt.

I've learned a lot about publishing in the last few months and if you are reading this, you know I have overcome another obstacle.

So, if you got this far, thank you for justifying my faith. I believe the information in this book will serve you well whether you make real estate a lifelong career or find yourself taking a different path. I don't advocate for or against real estate as a career choice, but I do try to create a better idea of what the challenges and solutions are.

You need to be curious; curious enough to want to read

everything remotely related to real estate, business, marketing, construction, architecture, and communication.

The characteristics that most often lead to long-term success in real estate are a love of people that is reflected by a large sphere of influence. You need to meet new people every day, and if that doesn't come easily to you, it will severely handicap your ability to grow your business.

Accomplishing important goals comes down to just a few individual traits: optimism, patience, faith, curiosity, and love. Oh, and of course, a sense of humor.

Here are 10 key ideas to form the core of your business.

1. **Never Stop Improving**

You, not real estate, are the product of your business. Keep making the product better.

2. **Building a business — not selling houses**

Do not become distracted from the daily commitments you have made to yourself to show property to a buyer who isn't loyal.

3. **Follow the business plan**

Potential buyers appear on the horizon and will attempt to lure you away from building a business and into the dark realm of the "ripe lead." Be wary of any potential leads that do not come from the seeds you planted.

4. **Focus on listing referrals, not buyers**

Stop looking for ripe buyers to pluck and start building a business, one relationship at a time.

CONCLUSION

5. **Meet people doing things you enjoy**

I saw recently where "Dirty Jobs" host Mike Rowe advised college graduates not to pursue their passions, which to me seems about the worst advice I have ever heard for someone entering a workplace where "jobs" themselves don't exist anymore.

I suppose there is a point to be made about the need to earn a living, reasonable expectations, and all of that self-limiting sort of thinking, but on the other hand, there are only about 675,000 hours in the average lifetime. About 200,000 will be lost to sleep and the rest is whittled away by personal maintenance tasks until there's only about 150,000 left, depending on how long you live. If you work forty hours a week for 45 years that's 93,600 hours and that time should be spent doing work you enjoy.

Mike Rowe is a wealthy TV star who subjects himself to some of the most dangerous and disgusting workplaces imaginable; literally work that you could not pay me to do so his advice on careers should be considered in that context.

To me, my passions have always led me where I was supposed to go, and I wish I had understood this earlier in life when I still thought like Rowe. We all have unique gifts and abilities that are intended to be pursued since they are the tools with which we have been equipped to make our way in this world. I think we are here to pursue our passions, not to spend our precious hours as a cog in the global corporate machine.

Rowe makes the point that if we suck at something, we have no choice but to abandon the passion. Here again, I disagree for a couple of reasons. The first is that most of us would not derive satisfaction from hopelessly failing over and over again. Second, practice makes perfect. If you are passionate, you will put in the time to excel.

Further, growing as we go through life is predicated on our ability to adapt. Remember, I wanted to be a baseball player, and here, Rowe's point would seem to apply. Looking back now, it is apparent that I earned a living playing ball all over the Southwest while meeting lots of like-minded people whom I cultivated as referral sources.

I'll tell you straight up that I am more than satisfied with the life I have lived and do not feel that I missed a thing. I played in thousands of games. I stayed fit, ate well to perform at my highest level, and had fun. And fun is the very best thing one can have.

6. **Real estate activity is driven by predictable life events**

Research tells us that it can be anywhere from several months to four years from the original idea to action. Salesmanship can't change that but patience and good follow-up will build your inventory and future earnings; that is how you build a business that is predictable — by tracking inventory.

7. **Do more CMAs — get more listings**

A few years ago, I was having lunch with a young associate and he mentioned to me that our waitress had thought about listing her house with him but decided to sell it by owner because she didn't think the proceeds, after closing costs, would be enough to really move up.

I asked him how much she needed to net on the sale. He didn't know. That became a teaching moment. He hadn't studied the market so he didn't even know what her proceeds would be. As it turned out, she had under estimated the sales price, and when she saw how much she would walk away with, she listed and the property quickly sold.

CONCLUSION

Make this the pillar of your business activity. Do a CMA for every homeowner you know at least once a year as a service to their financial planning. Sure, you could email it, but you are really doing reconnaissance so set an appointment and do your well-rehearsed presentation.

8. Rethink the open house opportunity

Most real estate agents dislike doing open houses since it is extremely rare, for a host of reasons, for a buyer to walk in off the street and buy that house from that agent. But, that isn't even the purpose. The purpose is to develop name recognition with potential first-time sellers in a neighborhood where you want to build a listing inventory. Open houses lead to CMAs if you conduct the open house to attract the neighbors.

9. Ethics in a competitive arena

Despite mandatory ethics training, the real estate business is so brutally competitive that ethics frequently takes a back seat to need and greed. Don't be that person! You have too much to lose. You not only risk your license, but you will lose yourself. There is nothing that adds more to one's level of confidence than knowing that you are fair and honest in all of your dealings.

10. One important question

Ask everyone you come in contact with, "Who do you know who might be thinking about selling their house?"

If you keep these key ideas in mind, you will have a much greater chance of building a rewarding business. Good luck!

APPENDIX A

MATCHMAKER OF SOUTHERN CALIFORNIA, Inc.

2515 Camino Del Rio South — Suite 202   San Diego, California 92108   Phone: 714-293-7590

August 1, 1979

Mr. George W. Mantor
9772 Caminito Doha
San Diego, CA 92131

Congratulations!

On a sunny Sunday where I encountered almost no one looking at open houses, I would like to take this opportunity to note and applaud the activity level at your Kendra Way property.

Whether due to your good directional signs, the well prepared appearance of the property, or the lure of the barbecue, you appeared to be doing an excellent job with legitimate prospects.

Of the many open houses visited Sunday, you seemed to be doing the most active job house sitting, and while I'm sure you are well satisfied with your present arrangement, I would like you to consider Matchmaker in the event you decide a change is in your best interests.

Matchmaker offers the advantages of both the large franchise operations and the giant independents, employing the best features of both, even to offering a profit-sharing plan to agents.

As Regional Director, I would be pleased to introduce you to Matchmaker brokers for additional information.

Sincerely,

John P. Fennell
Regional Director

JPF/clp

"Matching people with homes...all over America"
"Each office independently owned and operated"

APPENDIX B

The "Silver Corridor"
North County's Shining Future

By George W. Mantor
Broker/Owner
RE/MAX Buena Vista

Is the recession over? Who knows! It really doesn't matter. Recessions are like boats, the longer they are, the slower they turn. The effects, if any, are a long way off. But, in one north county region, long-range planning, inspired leadership, and persistence are already paying off.

Forget voo-doo economics, supply-side, trickle-down, the Laffer-curve, inflation, deflation, stagflation, recessions, depressions, up-tics, down-turns, and Clinton's campaign mantra, "It's the economy, stupid." It's time to stop blaming monetary policy, the budget deficit and especially that vague and murky culprit, the economy. Economies are results, not causes. The three most important issues are jobs, jobs, jobs.

Need more taxes? Or, as they say in Washington spin-speak, revenue increases. Put more people to work and tax revenues will increase. Want to reduce substance abuse? Make people productive. A reduction in substance abuse and a lower crime rate would translate into decreased health care costs. Resources would go further meaning better care for everyone.

Just as important, a working community has pride, confidence and compassion. That means better educated children, less fear, hate, and prejudice. Sounds good, doesn't it?

HIGH-VALUE JOBS

Indeed, the best thing that could happen to any community would be to find itself the destination of a major influx of high-value jobs. And, that is exactly what is happening within an area of less than 25 square miles, in North County's "Silver Corridor."

Running along highway 78 from Twin Oaks Valley Road to Melrose Drive, and extending south and west to include the South Vista Industrial area and Palomar Airport, the Silver Corridor includes parts of three cities and impacts several others.

Major employers include California State University at San Marcos, which will provide jobs in administration, academics, and a full range of maintenance and support jobs. Scripps and Kaiser hospitals will bring doctors, nurses, technicians, researchers, administrators, pharmacists, and maintenance workers. Businesses catering to patients, students, and employees will flourish, and associated bio-tech will be attracted to this area.

Wait! It gets better. These are the jobs of the future. With an aging population, health care is a major growth industry. This past September the University opened to an enrollment of more than 2,500 students. And in doing so, took the first step toward preparing north county residents to fill those jobs.

And, then, there's the Regional Justice System at 78 and Melrose Drive. A Brookings Institute study by Warren Cikins concluded that if America continued to incarcerate its residents at the current rate, half the population would be behind bars by the year 2053. It went on to presume that the other half would be working in the burgeoning correctional industry.

In the absence of an extraordinary decrease in the crime rate, this unhappy fact is also a cloud with a silver lining. The Vista facility is expanding from 23 to 84 courtrooms. At a cost of 200 million dollars, this attraction will bring law enforcement officers, bailiffs, para-legals, researchers, detectives, court reporters, judges, expert witnesses, jurors, and yes, even lawyers.

High-value, skilled jobs paying between $25,000-$75,000 per year are pouring into the "Silver Corridor," an area already blessed with a perfect climate, unparalleled views, rapidly improving transportation systems, and, for the moment at least, affordable housing.

For the first time in recent memory, the VA loan ceiling is sufficient to buy a median priced home. So are the incomes that will be derived from these jobs. Interest rates are at their lowest in two decades and there's plenty of inventory. And despite conventional wisdom that there is a steady stream of U-Hauls heading north and east, SANDAG reported that last year's influx of new residents increased from 22,678 in 1990-91 to 23,904 in 1991-92.

Still the gloom and doom persists and we continue to buy into it. The "Silver Corridor" is poised for the biggest real estate boom in its history and the only thing delaying that is us. If we're waiting for things to improve, it could be a long wait. We already have everything we need but we haven't been getting the message out. We are the industry with the most to gain and it is up to us to spread the message of the "Silver Corridor."

Reprinted from the April 1993 issue of The Vista Realtor News

APPENDIX C

What's Next For San Diego Real Estate?

George W. Mantor
"The Real Estate Professor"

July 25, 2009

North San Diego County HomeDex June 2009 Summary Report Single-Family Detached Homes

Month/Year	Median Home Prices		HomeDex (percentage of SD County households affording median priced homes)	
	North SD County	Non-North SD County	North SD County	Non-North SD County
June 2008	$490,000	$385,000	18%	27%
July 2008	$457,500	$376,500	21%	29%
Aug. 2008	$450,000	$360,000	20%	29%
Sept. 2008	$430,000	$350,000	22%	30%
Oct. 2008	$408,000	$345,000	24%	32%
Nov. 2008	$358,000	$325,000	31%	35%
Dec. 2008	$375,000	$335,000	29%	34%
Jan. 2009	$361,250	$310,000	29%	36%
Feb. 2009	$364,900	$320,000	34%	40%
Mar. 2009	$364,000	$305,000	34%	43%
Apr. 2009	$390,000	$310,000	31%	42%
May 2009	$397,000	$315,000	32%	38%
June 2009	$375,250	$326,750	30%	41%

North San Diego County Housing Characteristics
Single-Family Attached Homes
June 2009

Median Price	$255,000
Average Price	$285,082
Median Price per Square Foot	$207
Lowest-Priced Home Sold	$54,000
Highest-Priced Home Sold	$1,600,000
Number Units Sold	297
Total Sales	$84,669,210
Median Days on Market	43
Median Square Feet	1,180
Median Number of Bedrooms	2
Median Number of Baths	2
Median Age (years) of Homes Sold	27

North San Diego County HomeDex
June 2009 Summary Report
Single-Family Attached Homes

Month/Year	SFA Median Home Prices		HomeDex Single-Family Attached	
	North SD County	Non-North SD County	North SD County	Non-North SD County
June 2008	$266,000	$250,000	45%	48%
July 2008	$252,500	$246,000	48%	49%
Aug. 2008	$261,200	$232,000	45%	50%
Sept. 2008	$230,000	$228,000	51%	51%
Oct. 2008	$208,000	$201,000	56%	57%
Nov. 2008	$180,000	$203,000	63%	57%
Dec. 2008	$210,000	$195,000	56%	59%
Jan. 2009	$198,000	$190,000	59%	61%
Feb. 2009	$181,000	$189,000	67%	65%
Mar. 2009	$186,000	$170,000	66%	70%
Apr. 2009	$197,000	$175,500	64%	69%
May 2009	$216,000	$198,900	60%	64%
June 2009	$255,000	$191,500	53%	66%

APPENDIX C

San Diego Real Estate Dynamics
July 25, 2009

- **San Diego County:**
- Size: 4,261 square miles
- Number of Cities: 18

- **Orange County:**
- Size: 798 square miles
- Number of Cities: 34

- **Riverside County:**
- Size: 7,208 square miles
- Number of Cities: 26

- **San Diego Statistics:**
- Physical Characteristics: Cleveland National Forest, International border, Pacific Ocean, Camp Pendleton, Hills and Canyons, Indian Lands
- Population of County: 3,200,000
- Annual Growth Rate: 35,000-40,000
- Number of Households: 1,100,000
- Total Housing Stock: 1,150,000
- Single Family Detached: 552,000
- Single Family Multiple Unit: 133,000
- Multi-Family: 413,000
- Mobile Homes: 45,000
- Total Persons per Household: 2.8
  - Total Persons Per Household Nationwide: 2.59

Annual Listings and Sales in San Diego County

Year	Listings Taken	Sales Closed
2008	NA	34,182
2007	70,645	20,695
2006	76,721	28,977
2005	81,500	37,908
2004	64,529	40,126
2003	56,092	34,200
2002	58,426	36,549
2001	59,148	35,189
2000	55,777	36,568
1999	57,896	40,251

Ten year average annual Sales: 34,465

Monthly Average: 2,872

APPENDIX C

Sales in San Diego County for 2008 and May and June of 2009

- **San Diego Sales in 2008:**
- Number of Resale SFD: 20,695
- Number of Resale SFA: 9,792
- Number of New Sales: 3,725
- **Total Homes Sold in all of San Diego County in 2008:** 34,182
  - Monthly Average Sold in 2008: 2,849

- **San Diego County Homes Sold in May 2009:**
- Resale SFD: 2,064
- Resale SFA: 970
- New Combined: 188
- **Total for May:** 3,222

- **San Diego County Homes Sold in June 2009**
- Resale SFD: 2,296
- Resale SFA: 1,100
- New Combined: 282
- **Total for June:** 3,678

North San Diego County Housing Characteristics
Single-Family Detached Homes
May 2009

Median Price	$397,000
Average Price	$535,960
Median Price per Square Foot	$197
Lowest-Priced Home Sold	$90,000
Highest-Priced Home Sold	$14,000,000
Number Units Sold	779
Total Sales	$417,513,048
Median Days on Market	45
Median Square Feet	1,909
Median Number of Bedrooms	4
Median Number of Baths	3
Median Lot Size (sq. ft.)	8,940
Median Age (years) of Homes Sold	23

North San Diego County HomeDex May 2009 Summary Report Single-Family Detached Homes

Month/ Year	Median Home Prices		HomeDex (percentage of SD County households affording median priced homes)	
	North SD County	Non-North SD County	North SD County	Non-North SD County
May 2008	$515,000	$400,000	17%	26%
June 2008	$490,000	$385,000	18%	27%
July 2008	$457,500	$376,500	21%	29%
Aug. 2008	$450,000	$360,000	20%	29%
Sept. 2008	$430,000	$350,000	22%	30%
Oct. 2008	$408,000	$345,000	24%	32%
Nov. 2008	$358,000	$325,000	31%	35%
Dec. 2008	$375,000	$335,000	29%	34%
Jan. 2009	$361,250	$310,000	29%	36%
Feb. 2009	$364,900	$320,000	34%	40%
Mar. 2009	$364,000	$305,000	34%	43%
Apr. 2009	$390,000	$310,000	31%	42%
May 2009	$397,000	$315,000	32%	38%

North San Diego County Housing Characteristics
Single-Family Attached Homes
May 2009

Median Price	$216,000
Average Price	$254,664
Median Price per Square Foot	$191
Lowest-Priced Home Sold	$54,000
Highest-Priced Home Sold	$1,635,000
Number Units Sold	275
Total Sales	$70,032,523
Median Days on Market	36
Median Square Feet	1,118
Median Number of Bedrooms	2
Median Number of Baths	2
Median Age (years) of Homes Sold	25

APPENDIX C

North San Diego County HomeDex
May 2009 Summary Report
Single-Family Attached Homes

Month/ Year	SFA Median Home Prices		HomeDex Single-Family Attached	
	North SD County	Non-North SD County	North SD County	Non-North SD County
May 2008	$300,000	$280,000	39%	43%
June 2008	$266,000	$250,000	45%	48%
July 2008	$252,500	$246,000	48%	49%
Aug. 2008	$261,200	$232,000	45%	50%
Sept. 2008	$230,000	$228,000	51%	51%
Oct. 2008	$208,000	$201,000	56%	57%
Nov. 2008	$180,000	$203,000	63%	57%
Dec. 2008	$210,000	$195,000	56%	59%
Jan. 2009	$198,000	$190,000	59%	61%
Feb. 2009	$181,000	$189,000	67%	65%
Mar. 2009	$186,000	$170,000	66%	70%
Apr. 2009	$197,000	$175,500	64%	69%
May 2009	$216,000	$198,900	60%	64%

North San Diego County Housing Characteristics
Single-Family Detached Homes
June 2009

Median Price	$415,000
Average Price	$533,342
Median Price per Square Foot	$208
Lowest-Priced Home Sold	$50,000
Highest-Priced Home Sold	$9,000,000
Number Units Sold	765
Total Sales	$406,940,047
Median Days on Market	45
Median Square Feet	2,004
Median Number of Bedrooms	4
Median Number of Baths	3
Median Lot Size (sq. ft.)	8,900
Median Age (years) of Homes Sold	21

APPENDIX D

OCTOBER 11, 1993

RE/MAX Buena Vista,
GEORGE W. MANTOR
Broker /Owner
1611-A South Melrose Drive, # 134
Vista, Ca. 92083
(619-758-7045)

RE: Letter of reference regarding Mr. Mantor.

To Whom it may concern:

My wife and I don't usually write many letters of recommendation simple because we rarely work with or have people work for us who warrant this kind of action. However Mr. Mantor most certainly warrants our recommendation. Let me explain, back in 1989 we bought our first house. This was the time when people who were looking for a house had to make an offer right on the spot because another buyer was in line ready to snap the property up. If you bought during this time I'm sure you can remember the buying fever that was present. The prices and equity seemed to be just going up-up and up. The worst thing we thought could happen was that the real estate market would level off a little. Never did we feel that the property values would go down in California.

Things were fine until career changes forced us to sell our home and move closer to work. Well approximately 2 1/2 years and four realtors later we still owned our home. The first realtor was our friend and very competent. The next three were so called " million dollar sellers " each from one of the big agencies. The real estate market had gone bust and property was dropping in value every day. We were desperate and in need of some extraordinary help.

My wife and I received the kind of help we needed in George Mantor from RE/MAX, Buena Vista . I had done some business in another state and a RE/MAX Broker had handled the transaction. I was impressed by the way the broker handled my account and I asked her if it was possible to get a referral for a broker in the area of Vista, California. The broker said it was and when I returned to California George contacted me.

When George came to my house he was well dressed and mannered. I explained to him the situation we were in and that we were ready to take a sizable loss to sell the house.

THE AWFUL TRUTH ABOUT CAREERS IN REAL ESTATE AND WHAT TO DO ABOUT IT

George and I talked about the real estate market and about the price we probably would have to list the property in order to sell (approximately 20% lower than what we payed originally). I thought George would jump at the chance to make a quick dollar , but he surprised us and at the same time gained our respect. George stood up and told us that he wanted to check the surrounding " comps " and that he wanted to do some thinking for a way to eliminate or at least limit our loss before he said yes to listing our house.

The next day he came by and informed us of the possibility of selling our home under what was called a short sell or a compromise. Basically what the deal entailed was when we had an offer at a given price which was below what the amount of the loan was for, the lenders and the agencies guarantying the loan would step in and cover the difference. George explained that a short sell didn't always close and that the lenders or agencies involved didn't always agree to complete this type of deal, however he agreed to accept our listing.

Mr. Mantor in just four short months put together a listing on our house which included advertising, research, home presentation, and most importantly follow-up. His persistence and perseverance was instrumental in the successful selling of our home.   If I could put my finger on the most important element which sold our home I would have to say that it was George's timely follow-up. My wife and I never were at loss as to exactly where we were in the listing and escrow of our home.   George always made sure that we knew he was representing just us.

My wife and I could not praise the efforts of George W. Mantor enough. When you decide to have a RE/MAX Agent, Broker or Owner represent your interests you will be enlisting the efforts of a true consummate professional.   Make no mistake about it, George W. Mantor is at the cutting edge of his profession and it is with our pleasure that my wife and I present him with this letter of reference.

Once again, George thank you for letting my wife and I get on with our lives. Your efforts will not be forgotten.

Very truly yours,

Gerry Johnston
Gerry Johnston
Federal Bureau Of Investigation

Craig Johnston
Craig Johnston
Deputy Sheriff

Reference from Dan Maloney

I have the utmost respect and gratitude for George Mantor. I first met George in 1997 having just come back into the real estate field full time in 1994. I had come from a company who gave their agents leads based on a magazine that they had in racks at all the north county convenience stores. Prospective buyers would call based on their interest in listings in the magazine. It was a daunting task to go through 20 plus leads a day trying to find a real live buyer. It was very unsatisfying and inconsistent. I was ready to call it quits in real estate. However, a good friend of mine who had worked at the same company had recently gone over to the Keller Williams office that George owned and told me I should come and speak with George.

I met with George and shared my discouragement with the situation and my inability to produce at a sufficient level to support my family. George asked me to commit to a 12 week training program that he said would change my paradigm and ability to do real estate at a level that would transform my finances and also my life. He called it the "Success Workshop." He asked me to commit to being on time, attending each week and to doing what he asked me to do. I even had to sign a contract to that effect. After just a few weeks a light bulb came on in my mind and I knew I could be successful at this "business" of real estate. He taught me about the power in the people that I knew, my friends, relatives, past clients, people I did business with, people I associated with in my church, hobbies, interests and just about everyone I came in contact with. He taught me that they are all potential buyers or sellers and not only that but that they would most likely hear about 4-5 people in their sphere of influence that would be selling or buyer a home in the next year. His approach to finding buyers and sellers was completely different from the standard used by most real estate companies. What was being preached were things like door knocking, up time at the office reception desk, going to caravan meetings, passing your card out to everyone you meet, paying

THE AWFUL TRUTH ABOUT CAREERS IN REAL ESTATE AND WHAT TO DO ABOUT IT

for ads in newspapers, etc, etc. What George was teaching not only made sense, it worked. Two months into the training, I closed almost $30,000 in commissions. This was more than I had made the previous 10 months. By applying the methods and ideas George taught me I dramatically transformed my life, finances and most of all the way I related to doing business in real estate. George taught me to change the way I approached real estate. Instead of it being a job, he said "make it your business and become the President of it." He taught me how to keep track of the value and worth of my business which in turn kept me focused on which potential buyer or seller needed the most contact and attention. By creating a data base of all the people that I knew and making a concerted effort to contact them and give them my "Referral Contract." George called one of his methods "Touches." He taught that we had to keep in contact with our data base by "Touching" them with emails, letters, phone call, personal notes or face to face contacts.

Long story short, within a year I was a top producing agent in his office and from 1999 to present have been in the top 1% of agents nationwide for production. George Mantor has transformed my life and given me the understanding and tools to compete with large offices and so called mega agents with confidence and great success. I will be forever be indebted to George for showing me the way to do business in real estate and giving the ability to financially take care of

my family. I highly recommend George and his teaching, ideas and his great ability to help you understand the methods and paradigms he shares with willing to change their lives. Thank you George, you are truly the "Answer Man."

Sincerely yours,
Daniel Maloney, Broker/Owner, Daniel Team Realty

Reference from Crystal Pierce

In 2000 I was a single mom going to school to be a nurse and working part time at a mortgage company. It seemed like everyone was making money except me so I decided to get my real estate license. I was discouraged by a broker who told me that being a single mom it would be impossible for me to succeed.

Fortunately, I met an agent who encouraged me to attend an office meeting and assured me that his broker had a very different outlook and that I would likely have better results using his methods.

He favors business building concepts over prospecting and selling. He recommended a focus on listings rather than buyers. His time planning system stresses scheduling activities that we enjoy where we can grow our community of likeminded referral sources.

His tactics and ideas were not just to sell a house- but to live with integrity- to always do the right thing and put your client's needs first.

And most importantly he made it clear that I had a responsibility to my clients and to myself as a professional to devote regular time to pursuing mastery in all areas of my business.

George often stresses that real estate and money are connected. After I had built a foundation, George suggested that I learn the lending side of the business. At first- I was adamant- I would never do loans. I had no interest in it. And frankly, it seemed over my head but good coaches show us what we are capable of.

Being the one providing the money leads to absolute buyer loyalty.

THE AWFUL TRUTH ABOUT CAREERS IN REAL ESTATE AND WHAT TO DO ABOUT IT

The most important thing I learned as a single mom was how to block out my time so that the things that are most important, such as things involving my kids were scheduled first. Whatever is left is scheduled for real estate activities. That shows you how much time you really have because it isn't how much time you spend in your business but the urgency with which you tackle the important things like meeting people, making friends and asking for referrals.

I can honestly say that if it were not for George I would not be in the real estate business today.

Crystal Pierce

THE HASS TEAM REALTY

Oceanside, CA 92056

Reference from Pamela Seley

I became a real estate agent in 2007 right when the market tanked. While I made more money than my peers it wasn't nearly what I expected. It's harder than it looks.

George advises building one's value and so I learned the "short-sale" process. Everything I ever wanted to know about mortgage fraud I learned from doing short sales. Armed with a better understanding I was able to successfully negotiate mortgage debt relief for many unfortunate borrowers.

I persevered when so many told me I couldn't do it, and took on the responsibility to go get the education and training I needed to succeed, because what I needed to know was not going to be handed to me on a silver platter.

There is some luck involved--but what is luck other than being prepared when opportunity knocks?

Pamela Seley
Murrieta, CA 92562

Reference from Susan Stotler

My journey in Real Estate began in 1987 at the age of 20 when I obtained my California Real Estate Salesperson License.

One of my first mentors was George Mantor who instilled in me the necessity of working my sphere of influence. I became friends with my neighbors and children's parents who in turn entrusted me with representation in both listing and selling property. I discovered at a very young age, the value in creating close relationships and the necessity to listen closely. I was passionate about the needs of my clients. Within a very short time, I won top listing agent and #2 sales agent at an office that catered to top producers. From there my career took off and I was starting to receive name recognition in my community.

After two years of selling real estate, I decided to pursue my original career in mortgage banking that I started at the age of 18. The experience I gained in real estate sales gave me valuable insight into the truly difficult challenges real estate agents face. Countless hours of researching, driving and catering to clients without pay. I used my experience and relationships I created with other sales agents to become a top producer in the mortgage banking industry.

The bottom line is that real estate and mortgage banking are both service oriented relationship driven positions which require passion, patience and good listening skills. Without the original advice from my mentor, George Mantor I may not have started with my sphere of influence which was the key to my success.

Susan Stotler
Carlsbad, CA

ABOUT THE AUTHOR

George W. Mantor is a nationally respected authority in the field of real estate and is a frequent contributor to *Real Estate Finance*, *The Real Estate Professional*, *Real Estate Information Services Media*, *National Real Estate Investor*, *Broker Agent News*, and *Realty Times*. *The Real Estate Professional* includes him in "a directory of the Nation's outstanding authors, columnists, and speakers."

An oft invited guest of Fox Business Network, George is frequently quoted in a wide range of publications. For three years he was the host of "Keepin' It Real…Real talk about the real thing, real estate" on KCEO radio, and co-hosted "Real Estate Today" with Joe Tutino on KASH business radio.

Known as "The Real Estate Professor" for his consumer education efforts including a long-running radio program, monthly workshop series, public appearances and frequent articles, George has devoted his life to demystifying real estate.

He has amassed experience in new home and resale residential real estate, resort-marketing, and commercial and investment property for more than 35 years. In addition, he has served on virtually every real estate committee, including a term as director of the California Association of REALTORS.

During this period, George has developed solid relationships with industry leaders and has over a thousand connections between LinkedIn and Facebook.

George's career experience includes:

- Office manager for Walker and Lee Real Estate (became Great Western Real Estate), where he took the office from No. 79 in the company to No. 11 in bottom line profit in 18 months.
- Director of Training and Client Services for Bretcourt Financial Commercial Real Estate, where he marketed real estate related financial services to employees of Fortune 500 firms through retirement education workshops.
- In 1992, George became the owner and operator of a RE/MAX franchise.
- In 1997, George opened the first Keller William franchise in California and recruited 130 associates to the company
- From 2000 to the present, George has owned and operated his own consulting and brokerage firm, The Associates Financial Group. His emphasis has been on multi-family developments caught in the downturn or facing other unique obstacles.
- George's new condo project involvements include The Mercury in downtown Los Angeles, Atwater Place in Portland, Oregon, and the Ridge at Troon North in Scottsdale, Arizona.
- George has been a certified as real estate continuing education instructor by The California Bureau of Real Estate.

www.ingramcontent.com/pod-product-compliance
Lightning Source LLC
Chambersburg PA
CBHW070558300426
44113CB00010B/1304